RELIGION, EDUCATION,
AND THE
SUPREME COURT

RELIGION
EDUCATION
AND THE
SUPREME COURT

THAYER S. WARSHAW

Abingdon

Nashville

Religion, Education, and the Supreme Court

Library of Congress Cataloging in Publication Data

Warshaw, Thayer S   1915-
Religion, Education, and the Supreme Court.

1. Religion in the public schools--Law and
legislation--United States--Cases. I. Title.
KF4162.A7W37   344'.73'0796   78-11762
ISBN 0-687-36006-4

Manufactured by the Parthenon Press at
Nashville, Tennessee, United States of America

Preface

Years of teaching the Bible in secondary school and college literature courses brought two kinds of questions from educators and religious leaders: How is the teaching of literature, particularly religious literature, related to teaching about religion and to moral education? What does the law of the land forbid and what does it permit?

Experience with our institute for teachers at Indiana University suggested that satisfactory responses would require a fairly thorough examination of constitutional guidelines and their history. The general questions became more specific: What issues have arisen when the interests of American education met those of religion? What has the Supreme Court said about those issues? In partial answer, this book presents a broad array of problems, court cases, and Supreme Court actions related to the religion clauses of the First Amendment of the U.S. Constitution.

Chapter 1 offers background information for understanding the constitutional provisions. It also introduces some contemporary controversies in education that spring from our dual heritage—both the separation and the interaction of church and state.

Chapter 2 reviews relevant Supreme Court decisions and opinions over the past fifty years. Reviews of this kind may be organized either chronologically or topically but either approach should permit the other. Here the main thread is chronological; and to compensate, most case reports and discussions include references to other cases that deal with similar topics.

Certain issues result in key cases, which the reader may prefer to examine directly. For the question of prayer and Bible reading in public schools, see Engel (1962) and Schempp (1963). For aid to sectarian schools and/or their pupils and parents, see Everson (1947), Allen (1968), Lemon (1971), and Nyquist (1973). For aid to sectarian colleges, see Tilton (1971) and Roemer (1976). For a discussion of religion and moral education, see Welsh (1970).

This book is generally limited to the decisions and official opinions of the U.S. Supreme Court. It only glances at the many other relevant judicial, administrative, and legislative actions at all levels of government, from Washington to the local school building. Furthermore, the book is for laymen, by a layman. On both counts, specialists will want to go further.

Three recent books are particularly useful and readable: Religious Freedom, by Leo Pfeffer (National Textbook Company, 1977); The Wall of Separation, by Frank Sorauf (Princeton University Press, 1976); and Endangered Service, by the National Commission on United Methodist Higher Education (Nashville, 1976).

Most of the important earlier books are included in Church-State Relations: An Annotated Bibliography, by Albert J. Melendez (Garland Publishing, Inc., 1976). In addition, there are many valuable periodical publications by law schools, special interest groups, and commercial and professional enterprises.

People especially interested in teaching about religion or studying the Bible in public schools might examine two books: Teaching About Religion in Public Schools, by Nicholas Piediscalzi and William E. Collie (Argus, 1977), and Handbook for Teaching the Bible in Literature Classes, by Thayer S. Warshaw (Abingdon, 1978).

It is customary for an author, while assuming responsibility for inaccuracies and for infelicities of expression, to thank and absolve the typist. In this instance, the author must take the blame for the typing errors as well.

I wish to dedicate this book to Ellie, Shirley, and Maggie, who gladden the hearts of their parents.

Thayer S. Warshaw, Associate Director,
Indiana University Institute on
Teaching the Bible in Literature
Courses

FOREWORD

Few issues have been more divisive in our time than the role of religion in education. Often in the last three decades the Supreme Court has been called upon to arbitrate disputes that the political process could not, or would not, resolve. Chiefly, these disputes have arisen from governmental attempts to support or favor religious activity in ways that are nonsectarian and in most other nations would be unobjectionable. But our country has a special history and a special fear of proximity between government and religion. That fear is reflected in the clause of the First Amendment which forbids an "establishment" of religion and has been held by the courts to prevent much more than the endowing of an official state church. Indeed, the current interpretation of the First Amendment in such matters goes much further than the framers of the Constitution could have contemplated—since there were no public schools in their day—but is consistent with their concerns about the relationship of government and religion.

This book provides a valuable compendium of Supreme Court cases, with appropriate and welcome reference to important decisions of lower federal and state courts which the Supreme Court has declined to review. Both the introductory chapter and the case section remind us that the current controversy—which some now think traces from the prayer and Bible decisions of the early 1960's—really has much deeper roots, and that in fact the Supreme Court touched at least the periphery of the current dilemma almost a century earlier. Although the volume of litigation has increased markedly in the last quarter century—especially in the last decade or so—the antecedents are important and need from time to time to be recalled in the way this book does. The rationale of the two constitutional provisions dealing with religion—the clause which protects freedom of worship as well as the one which forbids establishment of religion—needs to be reviewed from time to time, as the background chapter carefully and conscientiously does.

This volume serves not only as a vehicle for understanding, but also as a tool for teaching about religion and education. The glossary is invaluable for the lay reader and reminds the lawyer that terminology may impede understanding in ways we seldom appreciate. The rich array of "issues for discussion" in the Appendix broadens the usefulness of the book as well; any class, at any level (including advanced students in constitutional law or in religion) could profit considerably from discussing some of the dilemmas and conflicts posed through these thoughtful questions. The dual function of the book thus contributes to its utility and makes it more than just a casebook or compendium.

The gravity and tension of the theme give the book vitality. This is—to borrow an apt statement from Dean Frank Sorauf's recent study—"the story of some of the most anguished constitutional controversies of the time. Only the furor over desegregation and the rights of racial minorities rivaled the intensity of feeling on prayer in the public schools, or public aid to private religious schools. These were not only constitutional questions of baffling complexity and closely matched equities. They were also issues of public policy to excite the most fervent beliefs and to test the resilience of American religious heterodoxy."

Robert M. O'Neil, Professor of Law
Vice-President, Indiana University,
Bloomington, Indiana

CONTENTS

RELIGION, EDUCATION,
AND THE
SUPREME COURT

Chapter 1. HISTORICAL BACKGROUND

A. The two religion clauses and the framers' pronouncements

In the preamble to the U.S. Constitution the framers listed the purposes of the federal government:

> To form a more perfect union, establish justice, insure domestic tranquility, provide for the common defense, promote the general welfare, and secure the blessings of liberty.

The Constitution went on to spell out the powers necessary to fulfill each of these purposes, but said little about the last one. Many people required a more complete and specific description of "liberty" and of how its blessings were to be secured.

Several states ratified the document only when assured that it would soon be accompanied by a bill of rights protecting individuals and states against the federal government. The First Amendment, adopted in December, 1791, guaranteed religious liberty and freedom of speech, the press, assembly, and petition. Unlike the last four areas of protection, religion had two "clauses":

> Congress shall make no law respecting an establishment of religion, or prohibiting the free exercise thereof.

The two religion clauses constitute history's first national "separation of church and state," to use Jefferson's interpretation of their meaning. The rigor with which our country examines that separation today still puzzles foreigners and, indeed, many of our own citizens.

[We shall be using the expressions "separation of church and state" and "religious liberty" interchangeably to epitomize the joint meaning of the two clauses, although some authorities make a distinction between the two labels.]

Over the years, the Supreme Court has unfolded the practical implications of these first sixteen words of the First Amendment. In the process, the Court has developed and refined criteria for deciding cases whose circumstances the framers of the Constitution may not have foreseen. In that sense, the Court's pronouncements have changed the "meaning" of the religion clauses. Naturally, controversy has attended both the begetting and the birth of such changes. Chief Justice Hughes went so far as to say, in another context, that "the Constitution is what the judges say it is."

It was nearly ninety years before the Supreme Court had to wrestle with the meaning of the religion clauses. When the Court did begin its history of interpretation, it had as background for its deliberations three major influences: 1) pronouncements of eminent earlier men, especially the framers; 2) laws of the individual states; and 3) customs of the people. The Court has gradually altered its attitude toward each of these traditions. Let us glance, in this section and the next two, at examples of each influence.

James Madison, author of the First Amendment, wrote in "A Memorial and Remonstrance Against Religious Assessments" (1784):

> We maintain, therefore, that in matters of religion no man's right is

abridged by the institution of civil society; and that religion is wholly exempt from its cognizance . . . It is proper to take alarm at the first experiment on our liberties . . . The same authority that can force a citizen to contribute three pence only of his property for the support of any one establishment may force him to conform to any other establishment in all cases whatsoever.

President Thomas Jefferson, who had been Madison's ally, wrote to the Danbury Baptist Association (1802):

I contemplate with sovereign reverence that act of the whole American people which declared that their legislature should "make no law respecting an establishment of religion, or prohibiting the free exercise thereof," thus building a wall of separation between church and State. [original capitalization]

It is significant that Jefferson should have used the "wall of separation" metaphor to a group of Baptists. Roger Williams, a religious refugee from Puritan Massachusetts, founded the new world's first Baptist church in Providence, Rhode Island, in 1639. He spoke of a "hedge or wall of separation between the garden of the church and the wilderness of the world."

Jefferson and Madison were deists, influenced by the anti-clerical Enlightenment, and were products of the relaxed Anglican establishment tradition. Although they strongly supported free exercise of religion, their main concern was to keep religion out of politics. As secular separationists, they wanted to protect the state from religion.

In contrast, the Baptists were religiously conservative; but they represented minorities that were equally zealous for church-state separation. Their emphasis, however, was quite different from Jefferson's. While they vigorously objected to the establishment of religion, their primary practical interest was in freedom to worship as they chose. As religious separationists, they wanted to protect religion from the state.

In an oversimplified sense, the two religion clauses represent these two interests. The two clauses provide freedom _of_ religion (free exercise) and freedom _from_ religion (no establishment). Together they help to "secure the blessings of [religious] liberty" promised in the preamble to the Constitution.

Sometimes the two aspects of religious liberty are complementary: If the majority cannot establish its religion, then minorities are free to exercise theirs. Taken as one, the two clauses assume that government is colorblind concerning religion—that they "prohibit classification in terms of religion either to confer a benefit or impose a burden," in one formulation.

Sometimes, however, the two clauses conflict with each other, and the Court has only the two alternatives—either to confer a benefit or to impose a burden on religion. Shall the government benefit religion by supplying chaplains for the armed forces or burden it by refusing to do so? (See a further discussion in section C, below.)

Not only must the Court on occasion decide whether to favor either free exercise or nonestablishment, but it must also decide the limits of the state's involvement with religion. Over the years, the barrier that separates church and state has come to be recognized more as a penetrable hedge than a solid wall. Church and state in America are not in fact absolutely separate, nor can they be; for example, municipal firemen must put out a fire in a church. They interact in many ways, some of which are listed below.

This interaction between government and religion is responsible for a divisive polarity which some people have called separationism versus accommodationism. The debate over whether the government should preserve, reduce, or expand its accommodation to religion has a long and continuing history.

Unfortunately, these differences become more intense because many people take their separationist or accommodationist position according to their personal religious commitment. Division along sectarian lines promotes the kind of public religious controversy that the religion clauses were designed to alleviate. For example, on most "no establishment" issues Roman Catholics are generally accommodationist whereas certain Protestant and Jewish groups regularly support separationist positions. On "free exercise" issues, the sectarian alignments may shift. We shall now briefly examine the backgrounds of the polarity—first separation, then accommodation.

B. Separation: the Fourteenth Amendment and state laws

At the time of ratifying the Constitution, most of the former colonies were just beginning to consider moving away from their traditions of established religions. Established Christian churches had privileges, exclusive to one sect or shared among two or three, that extended even to payment of the clergy from public funds and stipulations that religious offenses were civil crimes. As for denial of free exercise, some had gone so far as to ban Quakers, Catholics, Jews, and/or Baptists from residence on pain of death, to say nothing of voting or having a church of their own.

A few states provided relatively free exercise of religion and freedom from establishment. Rhode Island, Virginia, and Pennsylvania were the most liberal. Nevertheless, Jefferson and Madison had to fight hotly to maintain Virginia's recently enacted "tolerant laws," which were threatened, and to expand them into a true "religious freedom" act. Madison's "Remonstrance," quoted above, particularly influenced the legislature and some powerful religious interests. The two men carried the fight into the framing of the federal Constitution, although Jefferson was in France as ambassador during the convention.

The subsequent history of the religion clauses reveals an expanding awareness and acceptance of pluralism in America. What began as sectarian toleration and offers of privileges and exemptions has tended to become rights—for all kinds of religion and irreligion equally. The circle of legitimacy has widened. Established Protestant denominations accepted the legal equality of nonconforming Protestants, then Catholics and all Christians, then Jews and other theistic faiths, then nontheistic religions, and finally nonbelievers and atheists. But the movement has been slow, and practice has not kept pace with law of the land.

Adoption of the Constitution and the first ten amendments—the Bill of Rights—was a major federal step toward civil liberties; but it did not necessarily separate church and state in the individual states, nor was it so in-

tended. In matters of religion, the states were autonomous. In fact, one of
the reasons for including the word "respecting" in the Establishment Clause may
have been to prevent Congress from disestablishing churches that were privi-
leged at the time.

In 1833 the Supreme Court refused to hear a case (Barron) involving a challenge to an established state religion, on the ground that, as Justice Marshall
said, the First Amendment applied to the federal government but not to the
states. On the same ground, the Court dismissed an appeal (Permoli, 1845) involving free exercise of religion under state law.

The desire to protect former slaves after the war produced the Fourteenth
Amendment, which became law in 1868. Section 1 reads,

> All persons born or naturalized in the United States and subject to the
> jurisdiction thereof are citizens of the United States and of the State
> wherein they reside. No State shall make or enforce any law which shall
> abridge the privileges or immunities of citizens of the United States;
> nor shall any State deprive any person of life, liberty, or property
> without due process of law; nor deny to any person within its jurisdic-
> tion the equal protection of the laws.

Although the Due Process Clause came from the Fifth Amendment, the Fourteenth Amendment did not automatically extend the entire Bill of Rights to the
states. In many states, traditional Christianity was still officially considered "parcel of the common law," which was inherited from England. Nonbelievers and "heretics" were not equal before the law. For example, a person who
did not believe in divine retribution, here or hereafter, for giving false testimony could not be a witness in court proceedings in many states.

In 1925, after decades of internal conflict, the Supreme Court did say in a
free speech case (Gitlow) that

> freedom of speech and of the press—which are protected by the First
> Amendment from abridgement by Congress—are among the fundamental person-
> al rights and "liberties" protected by the due process clause of the
> Fourteenth Amendment from impairment by the States.[p.666]

*[Page numbers refer to the record of the case in United States Reports. For
the full citation, see Appendix D.]*

But not until 1940 (in Cantwell) did the Court rule that the religion clauses of the First Amendment were applicable to the states under the Fourteenth.
(The Court did not extend to the states the federal Constitution's prohibition
against religious tests for public office until 1961, in Torcaso.)

As a result of the Cantwell ruling, not only Congress but the states as well
are now prohibited by the U.S. Constitution from abridging their citizens'
freedom of religion and freedom from religion. By 1940, most states had already incorporated the First Amendment's principles into their constitutions
or statutes (in some cases, as a requirement for entering the union). Some of
these state laws were more specific and limiting than the federal Establishment
Clause, especially about not using public funds for sectarian purposes.

C. Interaction: the public interest; customs of the people

As we have just noted, the separation clauses were not originally intended to interfere with state laws. Neither were they meant, even at the national level, to inhibit other governmental interests spelled out in the Constitution, nor to disturb the many popular customs in which church and state interacted.

Religious liberty may be limited when it conflicts with these governmental interests: 1) to form a more perfect union (when does accommodation to sectarian education provoke political divisiveness?); 2) to establish justice (when does a concession to religious minorities do economic harm to an employer or to fellow employees?); 3) to insure domestic tranquility (when does evangelism or denunciation "disturb the peace"?); 4) to provide for the common defense (when do activist conscientious objectors impede a war effort?); 5) to promote the general welfare (when does a religious practice endanger the health or "moral fabric" of society?). In no area of interaction have the justices found final criteria for deciding issues. In individual cases they generally weigh the facts and balance the interests.

Guarantees of religious liberty are conditional, as with freedom of speech and of the press; but opinions differ about whether it is the same kind of conditionality. Is religion different from the other two and entitled to special consideration? Should a practice that would not be protected under freedom of speech or the press be allowed if it is a religious practice? The question has caused controversy among legal scholars and has often divided the Court. (See Ballard, 1944, and discussion under Barnette, 1943.)

The Constitution of the United States, in contrast to most state constitutions, did not appeal to God—a deliberate omission. Until the First Amendment, the document referred to religion in only three instances. One stressed separation: Article VI, Section 3, said,

> No religious test shall ever be required as a qualification to any office or public trust under the United States.

The other two assumed interaction of church and state. The Constitution was dated in "the year of our Lord, one thousand seven hundred and eighty-nine." And in Article I, Section 1, Sunday was excluded in counting the ten days within which the President might exercise the veto power. These assumptions are minor but symbolic.

The citizens of the new country were generally a religious (i.e., Protestant) people whose institutions presupposed a Supreme Being, to paraphrase later pronouncements of the Supreme Court. The Declaration of Independence appealed to the "laws of nature and of nature's God" and said that "all men are endowed by their Creator with certain unalienable rights." It ended with a "firm reliance on the protection of Divine Providence."

In the colonies, in the new states, and in the federal government, many practices tied religion and state together. Neither "free exercise" nor "no establishment" was absolute in the customs of the people. The interaction, or "involvement" (the Court's current expression), continues today.

Church and state must interact in some judicial matters. Courts decide disputes over religious property and contracts: Which faction owns the assets of a church? Must the minister be paid? Must a member be reinstated? And religion is a legitimate consideration in divorce proceedings and in child custody and adoption cases.

Here are examples where "no establishment" is not absolute—where the state gives religion special consideration through cooperation or "accommodation":

Chaplains provide services to armed forces; clergy work for the government at sessions of legislatures, in veterans' hospitals, and in penitentiaries; they perform legal marriages. The President declares national days of prayer and issues a proclamation on Thanksgiving Day. Christmas is a national holiday. Religious inscriptions adorn public buildings, and in 1954 the words "under God" became part of the pledge of allegiance to the flag. In 1865 Congress permitted the phrase "In God We Trust" to be used on certain coins. In 1955 this was extended to all currency, and in 1956 the phrase was adopted as the official U.S. motto. Our national anthem expresses faith in God. Postage stamps have carried religious pictures at Christmas. Several state flags bear crosses or other religious allusions: e.g., Mormon in Utah, and in Rhode Island the anchor of hope from Heb. 6:19.

In several states blasphemy is still a crime, at least on the statute books. Public funds aid church-controlled hospitals, orphanages, housing for the elderly, and homes for delinquent children. Public poor farms and old age homes have publicly constructed chapels. Public funds provide sectarian schools with lunches, bus transportation, textbooks, and health and diagnostic services. At sectarian colleges the government funds secular programs, new buildings and equipment, and GI veterans' education—both secular and religious. Churches use public school buildings after hours, as when a sanctuary is being rebuilt. Evangelists speak in public, tax-supported parks.

Furthermore, religious beliefs exempt some people from military service; from social security taxes, welfare rules requiring Saturday work, and state Sunday closing laws; from vaccinations, the school flag salute, and attendance at high school; from oaths in court and jury duty; and from laws against hallucinogenic peyote. Most church property and income are tax exempt, yet churches receive police and fire protection and other municipal services. Churches may be built in most residential areas despite zoning ordinances. Clergy pay no taxes for rental of a parsonage, and contributions to religious institutions are tax deductible. In many instances, the state has not taxed commercial ventures operated by churches. Public utilities contribute to religious charities and pass on the cost to their customers.

Conversely, the state limits "free exercise":

The government prohibits polygamy and snake handling by religious sectarians. It orders fluoridation of water, chest x-rays, vaccinations against infectious disease, blood transfusions, and operations to preserve life even if these practices violate religious beliefs. The state may license religious demonstrations; limit religious freedom in the armed forces in wartime; require church deeds to be registered; and subject churches to fire inspections, building codes, and most zoning rules as well as regulations against pollution of the environment.

The state regulates academic, health, and attendance standards of church-sponsored schools. It prohibits public prayer and devotional Bible reading in public schools regardless of the wishes of the local majority. In some states, parents may not insist on a particular religious training for their child after the age of 12 or 13. The state prohibits parents from "abusing" their children physically or psychically in the name of religion. They may not violate child labor laws or keep children from all schooling for religious reasons.

The Internal Revenue Service determines what organizations are churches for purposes of tax deductions, and it limits the deductibility of gifts and bequests to religious institutions. The military decides who qualifies for religious conscientious objector exemptions. Prison wardens decide which prisoners may have religious privileges. States decide whether a particular group may incorporate as a religious organization and whether to accredit a sect's seminary. Courts decide whether a religiously discriminatory bequest to a public institution is valid. Some states define the boundaries between, and therefore limit, spiritualism (which may be considered a religion) and communicating with the dead or fortune telling (which may not). Other states prescribe the boundaries between religious faith healing (which is not regulated) and the practice of medicine (which is). A religious group may lose its tax exemption.

A minority may be inconvenienced by the majority: e.g., kosher butchers, closed on Saturday, may be forced to close on Sunday also. On the other hand, the religious sensibilities, if not the religious freedom, of the majority must give way to the religious freedom of a local minority: e.g., to accommodate the observance of Good Friday or Yom Kippur, a school administrator may adjust the school schedule if the minority is large enough. Poor people who insist on a religious education for their children face the inconvenience (or heavy burden) of additional tuition besides paying the public school tax.

These are instances of the interaction of church and state, in which the government either gives special consideration to religion or imposes limitations upon it. Most of the practices enumerated above have been or are the subject of controversies that have resulted in court decisions, legislative enactments, and/or administrative regulations at various levels of government.

Jefferson's "wall of separation" and Madison's "three pence" were for a long time thought to call for absolute separation of church and state, at least in theory. Jefferson sent his letter to the Danbury Baptists to explain his refusal to proclaim religious holidays. Madison objected to chaplains in Congress and in the army. But not all separationists followed theory with practice so closely. Interaction was the custom, and religion was part of American culture.

More recently, the Court has had to face up to challenges against historically accepted practices and to deal with increasingly complicated cases. It has acknowledged that the Establishment Clause and the Free Exercise Clause tend to conflict with each other if they are both taken as absolute. For example, the Walz case (1970) considered the problem of tax exemptions for church property used for religious purposes. The power to tax is the power to inhibit the scope of religion and its free exercise. Conversely, tax exemption is an indirect support of religion by the state. The Court admitted that

> either course, taxation or exemption, occasions some degree of [state] involvement with religion.[p.674]

The Court decided that the involvement was not great and approved exemptions.

Where rigid construction of the Establishment Clause would seriously limit free exercise, the Court has increasingly taken a benevolent attitude toward religion. But where the claims of free exercise call for so much state involvement that benevolence smacks of establishment, the Court steps back. The Nyquist case (1973), among others, considered the claim that poor people could not exercise freedom to choose religious education over public education if the state denied financial aid. The Court decided that the involvement was too entangling and denied the claim.

In sum, like all constitutional rights, religious liberty is not absolute. If taken as absolutes, the two clauses tend to conflict with each other, with the customs of the people, and with other claims of public interest. Jefferson's wall is in danger of becoming "as winding as the famous serpentine wall designed by Mr. Jefferson for the University [of Virginia] he founded," in the words of one justice. Certainly, some bricks have fallen or been knocked out, leaving large breaches. Separationists seek to maintain and strengthen the metaphorical wall; accommodationists want to tear down the metaphor along with the wall.

D. Two historic issues: Bible reading and "parochiaid" to Catholic schools

The Supreme Court has had to feel its way in applying the religion clauses to the schools. There were no public schools when the First Amendment was written. Once begun, they developed quite rapidly and they stimulated controversy. Two groups of issues stand out. Justice Powell, in Nyquist (1973), said,

> Most of the cases coming to this Court raising Establishment Clause questions have involved the relationship between religion and education. Among these religion-education precedents, two general categories may be identified: those dealing with religious activities within the schools, and those involving public aid in varying form to sectarian educational institutions.[p.772]

In the former category, the landmark decisions were separationist, disallowing compulsion to salute the flag (Barnette, 1943), released time religious education (McCollum, 1948), and prayer (Engel, 1962) in the public schools. Subsequent decisions have generally maintained this separationist stance.

In the latter category, the landmark case is Everson (1947). Its precedent-setting definition of the Establishment Clause was separationist; but its specific ruling was accommodationist: government might provide transportation for sectarian school pupils. Since then, the Court has followed this ambivalence, striking down some practices and permitting others.

Here is some background for representative issues in the two categories:

12

Bible Reading

State governments in America have always supported education as a part of their interest in "promoting the general welfare," in the language of the preamble to the federal Constitution. (The states' power to enact general welfare laws is called their "police power.") They must produce good citizens: an informed, critical, and responsible electorate that is committed to pluralistic democracy and that values love of country and respect for law. Without such a commitment, without such values, America is in danger.

These civic virtues are basic if we are to make progress toward a "more perfect union . . . justice . . . domestic tranquility . . . and common defense." Americans may tend to impose on education an unfairly large portion of the responsibility for forming young people's character, but education must assume at least its share of the burden. Thus, every state offers free public education, and all but Mississippi have seen fit to enact compulsory school attendance laws.

Originally, all schools were church-related. Religious belief and practice were considered essential to good citizenship, if not synonymous with it. Few people saw much distinction between the interests of church and state in the schools. (One of the few was Jefferson, who argued unsuccessfully for secular public schools.)

Even with the advent of public schools—an American innovation—separation of church and state proceeded very gradually. In fact, doubts about the wisdom of complete separation are lively today: Can morality be separated from religion? If so, should it be? Do public schools foster secularism? Should they? Reasonable people disagree or give qualified answers.

The story of morning devotional exercises in schools (prayers, hymns, Bible reading) reflects the developing separationism, and secularization, of public schools; and it points up present day concerns. Those interested in the history of Bible reading in public schools point to a milestone erected by Horace Mann, "father of the common school." In the late 1830's and the 1840's, he was secretary of the nation's first state board of education, in Massachusetts. Mann faced the problem of mandatory school Bible reading. (Until 1910, Massachusetts was the only state to have such a law, although the practice was widespread.) Various denominations were questioning the manner in which teachers conducted the devotions.

Mann's widely copied rule called for reading the Bible without comment, for the moral instruction of pupils in the commonly shared Christian values:

> Government should do all it can to facilitate the acquisition of religious truth, but shall leave the decision of the question what truth is, to the arbitrament, without human appeal, of each man's reason and conscience.

This rule was a major step toward separation of church and state in education. It tended against establishment by aiming at a nonsectarian stance, though it also inclined to favor the Protestant doctrine of the inviolability of conscience and it expected schools to use the King James Bible, both of which notions were unacceptable to Catholics. Even when expanded to include Catholics, however, Mann's rule assumed that the Bible and its teachings were not sectarian but "American." By the same token, the Christian faith, taken in all its denominations, was equally considered to be American and not sectarian.

The U.S. Supreme Court has since denied both of these assumptions, notably in Schempp (1963): The Bible is sectarian, and Christianity is only one of the American religions. The Schempp opinion repeated an even broader pronouncement of the Court: Not only does the Constitution prohibit government preference of any one religion over others, but it also forbids the advancement of religion in general over irreligion (Everson, 1947).

Although the Court has spoken and its rulings are the law of the land, not everyone agrees with or even obeys its decisions. Many people today echo Justice Brewer, who spoke for the Court fifty years after Mann. In Holy Trinity (1892), a Sunday observance case, he declared that "this is a Christian nation."[p.471] Still later, in Macintosh (1931), a naturalization and conscientious objection case, the Court said, "We are a Christian people."[p.625] More broadly, many religious spokesmen and legal scholars insist today that the Court was wrong to rule against aid to religion in general, despite the Court's frequent reaffirmations of its position.

Until Engel (1962), which outlawed nonsectarian school prayers, some state supreme courts were making statements similar to Brewer's. The Engel decision produced an uproar from many religious forces in the country. Many Christians still feel not only that the Bible is nonsectarian but also that its teachings constitute the American moral and spiritual values. The drive to reinstate inspirational Bible readings in the schools continues, although the Court is adamantly opposed and legislatures have not joined the drive.

The Court has yet to rule directly on another of Mann's unquestioned assumptions: the inseparability of "moral instruction" and religious indoctrination. "Conscience," in his rule quoted above, meant a religious, theistic attitude (as it did later in "conscientious objector"). Morality issued from religion. Humanistic, nonreligious conscience was not contemplated.

Interestingly, some people today also deny the existence of "nonreligious conscience," but on different grounds: They consider any purely humanistic and personal conscience to be one's religion. Others, with Dewey, speak of a national religion of democracy apart from conventional, organized religion. The effect of these two attitudes, as with Mann's assumption, is to blur the distinction between religious indoctrination and moral education.

That blur creates a dilemma for public education. In pursuit of the general welfare, the nation's schools must provide moral instruction, which many people consider to be inextricably tied to religion—whatever its definition. (See discussion under Welsh, 1970.) Where the Court once said, "we are a Christian people," it now says, "we are a religious people" (Zorach, 1952). And not merely a religious people, but a theistic people, "whose institutions presuppose a Supreme Being": For years now, one survey after another has reported that over 90% of Americans—more by far than in any other country—say they believe in God.

Parochiaid to Catholic schools

[Some separationists use the word "parochiaid" for its polemical connotation

14

of aid to Catholic schools, an implication that this book does not share. Nevertheless, this book does use the term as a convenient and affectively neutral way of denoting all kinds of direct or indirect public aid to sectarian education—to schools, colleges, students, or parents—of whatever denomination.

[True, the overwhelming majority of the country's nonpublic schools are Catholic: 92% of the sectarian schools and 87% of all nonpublic schools in 1965-66, the peak year for Catholic schools. But Lutherans, Jews, Adventists, Baptists, Mennonites, Congregationalists, Quakers, Episcopalians, and other groups maintain religious alternatives to the public school system. At the college level, there is even greater diversity—of sponsorship and degree of religiosity. (Some denominations, however, refuse parochiaid on principle, at both levels.)

[The broad category is nonpublic schools. Some are nonsectarian, independent, private schools—commercial or nonprofit. (Sometimes the word "private" is used as a synonym for all nonpublic schools or colleges.) Other nonpublic schools are sectarian, religious—including the Catholic ones, many of which are parochial, or parish, schools. Thus "parochiaid" as a generic term involves more than Catholic parish schools. Furthermore, we apply the word to aid that is aimed not just at the school itself but directly at its pupils—a benefit that the Court has accepted as not being an unconstitutional aid to religion, even though it may help the school indirectly. Thirdly, we also apply the term "parochiaid" to sectarian colleges, where the Court has approved much broader public support than for sectarian elementary and secondary schools.]

From earliest times, public funds supported religiously oriented schools in America. But in 1825 New York City's share of the state school funds went exclusively to the Free School Society, founded twenty years earlier

> for the education of such poor children as do not belong to, or are not provided for by any religious society.

This allocation paved the way for restricting governmental support of education to public, or "common," schools. The rapid spread of public schools that soon followed, patterned after Horace Mann's nonsectarian principles, collided with the first major influx of Catholic immigrants.

Two main factors account for the urge to establish Catholic schools in this country. First, Catholic immigrants reacted against the rampant Protestant and nativist antagonism toward Catholicism and Catholics that was reflected in the public schools, particularly evident in textbooks and in classroom discrimination. Catholic leaders appealed to the constitutional guarantees of the religion clauses for relief, with some success but often drawing violent reaction.

Second, and equally important, Catholic leaders were greatly concerned for the religious education of their children. Early complaints against sectarianism in public schools gave way to complaints against their secularism. Ironically, by showing the Protestant establishment that public schools were illegally sectarian, Catholics contributed to the schools' eventual secularization. Nor could attempts at nonsectarian religious or moral education satisfy devout Catholics, even when "nonsectarian" meant "interdenominational Christian." The 1929 papal encyclical "On the Christian Education of Youth" included among its pronouncements the following:

> The only school approved by the Church is one where . . . the Catholic

religion permeates the entire atmosphere.

The extent of that permeation has been a crucial issue in the Court's parochiaid decisions in the past decade.

Proponents of parochiaid to religious schools insist on the separability of secular aspects of Catholic (and other sectarian) education. This represents a shift in emphasis. Originally, some argued that because of the secularization of the public schools, only religious schools could perform the state's demand for moral education, and the state should therefore support sectarian schools. More recently, most proponents have argued that sectarian schools are entitled to public funds because they perform a separable secular educational function for the state.

Opponents of parochiaid challenge that separability. They point out that the 1929 encyclical is still in effect for Catholic schools, at least officially, and that it was reinforced by the Second Vatican Council's description of one of the purposes of sectarian schools: "to relate all human culture eventually to the news of salvation." Further, a Vatican statement of March, 1977, speaks of

> the difference between a school whose education is permeated by the Christian spirit and one in which religion is only regarded as an academic study, like any other. . . . The Catholic school differs from all others which limit themselves to forming men. Its task is to form Christian men.

In 1897 Congress adopted a non-binding declaration of policy: that the federal government "shall make no appropriation whatever for education in any sectarian schools." About the same time—when Catholics were actively pressing for public funds for parochial schools—several states amended their constitutions to include a similar prohibition.

Nearly every state today has some form of constitutional provision that limits or prohibits the expenditure of public money for sectarian education. Some of them erect a higher wall of separation than that of the federal Constitution as interpreted by the Supreme Court; they explicitly forbid even indirect aid to religion.

Thus, what the Supreme Court permits (e.g., busing, textbook loans) a state may forbid. Permission is not a mandate. In Brusca (1972), the Court ruled against an attempt to declare that such a state restriction was an unconstitutional violation of the Free Exercise Clause. The Court said the state had the right to deny benefits to pupils of religious schools. When Congress enacted the National School Lunch Act, to be administered by the states, some states did not include sectarian schools in the program.

The fullest discussion of the Court's position will be found under Nyquist (1973), but here is a brief resumé. Thus far (summer, 1978), the Court has approved state supported busing (Everson, 1947) and the loan of textbooks (Allen, 1968). These are pupil benefits. Schools themselves are allowed nonreligious health, diagnostic, and testing services (Walter, 1977). The Court has struck down many other plans, but pressure continues in the state legislatures and in Congress. (For college parochiaid, see Tilton, 1971, and Roemer, 1976.)

E. Three relevant early cases: Reynolds, Bradfield, and Meyer

Reynolds

(This case was not aimed at an educational issue, but it has implications for education because it first defined the meaning of the religion clauses and limited free exercise.)

In Reynolds v U. S. (1878), Mormons in the federally governed Territory of Utah challenged a statute that made bigamy a crime, but they lost their case. Speaking for the unanimous court, Chief Justice Waite paid his respects to Madison's "Remonstrance" and then officially endorsed Jefferson's "wall of separation" as the intended and proper interpretation of the religion clauses:

> Coming as it does from an acknowledged leader of the advocates of the measure, it may be accepted almost as an authoritative declaration of the scope and effect of the amendment. [p.164]

He noted, however, that Jefferson was convinced that mankind "has no natural right in opposition to his social duties." Thus Waite distinguished between belief and practice within the free "exercise" of religion. Through the First Amendment, he said,

> Congress was deprived of all legislative power over mere opinion, but was left free to reach actions which were in violation of social duties or subversive of good order. [p.164]

For example,

> Suppose one believed that human sacrifice were a necessary part of religious worship, would it be seriously contended that a civil government under which he lived could not interfere to prevent a sacrifice? [p.166]

[This choice of example tempts one to pose a frivolous question: Is bigamy a form of human sacrifice? And on whose part?]

The Reynolds case was the first occasion for the Court to interpret the Free Exercise Clause—nearly ninety years after its adoption. Not for another seventy years did the Court give its initial exposition of the Establishment Clause, in Everson (1947). There also the Court leaned heavily on Jefferson's "wall of separation."

Since Reynolds, the Court has restrained the principle of state regulation of religious practices. It protected Jehovah's Witnesses who antagonized the local majority, in Cantwell (1940) and in Barnette (1943)—in both of which cases free exercise of religion was combined with the issue of free speech. It also protected Mennonites, in Yoder (1972), against the state's insistence upon a high school education. But the principle remains strong: free practice of religion is not an absolute right.

Accordingly, several state constitutions have limitations on the freedom of religious practice. In Jacobson v Massachusetts (1905), the Court upheld the right of a state, as part of its "police powers," to require vaccinations regardless of religious scruples that were claimed to be personal "liberties" guaranteed under the Fourteenth Amendment. (This power of the state to require vaccinations has not been challenged under the First Amendment, although several states grant exemptions from vaccinations in specified instances.)

In Pack v Tennessee (1976), the Court unanimously refused to review (and thus left in effect) a ruling of the state supreme court that snake handling and the drinking of poison as part of a religious ritual may be prohibited as a "clear and present danger" to lives of others in the church and to the wor- shiper himself/herself. The state court said that "the state has a right to protect a person from himself."[527 SW2d p.113] *[For the meaning of the Court's refusal to review a case, see discussion under Doremus (1952).]* And as recently as 1946 (Cleveland), the Court reiterated its disapproval of bigamy.

The Court has tightened Waite's criteria for limiting religious practices. There must be a "clear and present danger of substantial injury to others"; or the practice must pose a "substantial threat to public safety, peace or order"; or it must obstruct a "compelling interest of the State" that cannot be achieved by any alternative means. Secular regulation of religious practices, in short, is not to be applied any more lightly than is limitation of free speech or the press. (See discussion under Cantwell, 1940; Sherbert, 1963; and Yoder, 1972.)

Although Reynolds was not an education case, the principle that religious practices are not absolutely free has implications for the classroom and lec- ture hall. Both students and teachers may be limited in their practices, even in expressions of belief if such expression violates one of the criteria.

As recently as 1955 the Court refused to review a ruling of a lower court that took children away from a mother in Utah (in re Black). She had "neglect- ed" her children by, among other things, teaching them that polygamy was God's will. (The court also considered her to have provided an "immoral"—i.e., po- lygamous—home unfit for children.) As for what one may teach in the matter of social duties, see Pierce (1925).

Bradfield

(This case involved an incidental application of the First Amendment religion clauses that also was not directed at an educational issue. It has implica- tions for education because it limited nonestablishment, even though the Court did not define the meaning of the Establishment Clause.)

In Bradfield v Roberts (1899), the Court held that a federal construction grant to a hospital operated by members of a (Catholic) religious order was not unconstitutional.

The hospital was incorporated and conducted for nonsectarian and secular, not for religious, purposes. The influence of the church over its incorpora- tors did not extend to the operation of the hospital. In fact, a major func- tion of the building was to serve publicly supported poor people who could choose their own nurses and doctors. The Court, speaking through Justice Peck- ham, considered the case a matter of corporation law.

Lawyers and judges have cited the Bradfield decision as a precedent that the Establishment Clause, like the Free Exercise Clause, is not absolute. Certain kinds of aid to church-affiliated or church-sponsored institutions are permis- sible if they serve a secular function: e.g., college buildings not used for religious purposes (Tilton, 1971, and Hunt, 1973).

Congress has also used this principle to justify the appropriation of federal funds for church related hospitals, elderly housing, and colleges. For example, under the Hill-Burton Hospital Survey and Construction Act of 1946, funds were given to the same hospital that was involved in Bradfield (and were challenged anew).

In subsequent religion cases, Bradfield was not important while the doctrine of the "wall of separation" was strong. It has come to the fore recently, as the Court has acknowledged the secular character of many church-sponsored colleges. The Court draws a line between the primary or principal secular effect of a law or practice and any merely incidental, indirect, or remote benefit to religion.

Meyer

(This case involved an educational issue that did not primarily concern religion, but turned out to have religious implications.)

In Meyer v Nebraska (1923), the Court struck down, 7-2 *[the greater the majority, the more likely the decision and opinion are to be appealed to as authoritative]*, a state law that prohibited the teaching of, or in, a modern foreign language before the ninth grade.

At issue was the teaching of German-language Bible stories in Lutheran and Reformed parochial schools. (The act included an emergency enforcement clause; Germany had been our recent enemy.) The state asserted its interest in the curriculum of independent schools through its right to insist on the proper education of all children. The Court held the statute to be an unreasonable deprivation of liberty within the terms of the Fourteenth Amendment.

Speaking for the Court, Justice McReynolds in his "obiter dicta" *[incidental remarks explaining the ruling and having less strength as a precedent]* acknowledged that

> the power of the state to compel attendance at some school and to make reasonable regulations for all schools . . . is not questioned. [p.402]

And no Supreme Court litigant successfully questioned compulsory attendance until Yoder (1972). The power to regulate curriculum in nonpublic schools, both secular and religious, has not been challenged before the Court. In 1976, however, the Ohio supreme court ruled that the state's "Minimum Standards for Ohio Elementary Schools" was unconstitutional as applied to nonpublic schools because the document's requirements effectively inhibited attempts by any school to engage in religious indoctrination. This ruling was not appealed.

Religious liberty was not an issue in Meyer because the Court had not yet ruled that the Free Exercise Clause of the First Amendment applied to the states through the Fourteenth Amendment. In passing, however, the Court pointed in that direction. Without doubt, its opinion noted, the term "liberty" in the phrase "deprivation of liberty" within the Fourteenth Amendment denotes

> the right of the individual . . . to worship God according to the dictates of his own conscience. [p.399]

But it was another fifteen years before the Court based a decision on that principle and made it official doctrine, in <u>Cantwell</u>.

Chapter 2. SUPREME COURT CASES

INTRODUCTORY NOTE: This chapter contains three kinds of material, differentiated by their appearance:

1. Roman type represents straight reporting of a case. This material is intended to be factual and objective, with comments aimed only at clarification. Its only conscious bias is the selection of those aspects of a case that are relevant to issues of religion and education.

2. Indented material in the same type is quoted from the justices' opinions, generally those that present the Court's official position. A bracketed page number following a quotation refers to the U.S. Report (or other report when so noted) where the case is recorded. See index of cases, Appendix D.

3. *Italicized material, within square brackets, is authorial comment and/or information beyond the case at hand. Thus, although most of the cases appear in chronological order, many of them contain references to other cases that are related topically.*

*   *   *

Pierce

In Pierce v Society of Sisters, 1925, the Court unanimously struck down an Oregon law that compelled all children to attend public schools. The law was appealed jointly by a Catholic school and an independent military academy.

Justice McReynolds, speaking for the Court (i.e., official author of the majority or prevailing opinion), cited the Meyer (1923) decision. He expanded its obiter dicta:

> No question is raised [by the schools] concerning the power of the State reasonably to regulate all schools, to inspect, supervise and examine them, their teachers and pupils; to require that all children of proper age attend some school, that teachers be of good moral character and patriotic disposition, that certain studies plainly essential to good citizenship be taught, and that nothing be taught that is manifestly inimical to the public welfare. [p.534]

However, he said,

> The fundamental theory of liberty upon which all governments in this Union repose excludes any general power of the State to standardize its children by forcing them to accept instruction from public teachers only. The child is not the mere creature of the State; those who nurture him and direct his destiny have the right, coupled with the high duty, to recognize and prepare him for additional obligations. [p.535]

[As in Meyer, it was the Fourteenth Amendment that was in question. The complaint charged deprivation of liberty of parents to buy education and of private enterprises to sell it. Even though both cases involved religiously oriented schools, the Court had not yet interpreted the Fourteenth Amendment so as to apply the religion clauses of the First Amendment to the states. (Nor was free speech the decisive issue, as it would be in future cases.) It was a matter of freedom to contract: property values, not civil liberties, were

...ed in both *Meyer* and *Pierce*.

...two decisions declared unconstitutional two similar laws against non-public schools. Both laws grew out of the exaggerated patriotism of World War I, which encouraged "native, white, Protestant" supremacy and saw a resurgence of the anti-foreign, anti-Negro, anti-Catholic, anti-semitic Ku Klux Klan.

[The Court's remarks about the "good moral character and patriotic disposition" of teachers and about "studies plainly essential to good citizenship" are of interest to people concerned with the teaching of values in public schools. In keeping with the government's interest in "promoting the general welfare," the Court has repeatedly acknowledged the schools' right and responsibility toward the (secular) promotion of moral values. Which of one's values are religious values depends on one's definition of religion. (See discussion under Welsh, *1970.)*

[The Court has not specified criteria of a teacher's good moral character, but religious tests are unconstitutional. And criteria for what may be taught are as uncertain as those for who may teach. At what point teaching becomes "manifestly inimical to the public welfare" can be a matter of considerable debate among professional educators and other people interested in education. (See discussion under Barnette, *1943.)*

[Later First Amendment religion cases appealed to Meyer *and* Pierce *as precedents. But the Court has never had to decide the specific issue of the right of sectarian schools to existence and to protection on First Amendment grounds. The Court's strong dicta in these two cases have been widely respected. Local authorities have, however, denied permits to churches that wanted to operate a school in a residential area, a ruling recently challenged in Oregon.]*

Cochran

In *Cochran* v *Board of Education*, 1930, the Court unanimously approved the free loan of textbooks to children in Louisiana religious schools, provided that the books were the same as used in public schools, the content was secular, and they were used for secular purposes.

Again, it was the Fourteenth Amendment that was at issue. Cochran charged that the practice violated the Deprivation of Private Property / Due Process Clause and the Equal Protection Clause. It took private property (money) without due process (by taxation) for the unequal (private) use of others rather than for public purposes, he charged. *[The program was part of the flamboyant Governor Huey Long's populist public welfare activities.]*

The Court denied the charge and ruled that the practice was not unconstitutional, as Cochran had claimed: "The taxing power of the state is exerted for a public purpose"—education.[p.375] The decision did not consider whether such a loan violated the separation clauses of the First Amendment. *[That finally was the issue in the textbook loan case of* Allen *(1968).]*

Speaking for the Court, Chief Justice Hughes agreed with the state supreme court's opinion, which said that the books were not bought for schools but for children [p.375]:

The schools, however, are not the beneficiaries of these appropriations
. . . The school children and the State alone are the beneficiaries.

[This is the first mention, though peripherally, of the "child benefit" theory as distinguished from direct support of sectarian schools. The theory figures strongly in the landmark Everson busing case (1947) and in later cases.]

Hamilton

In Hamilton v Regents of the University of California, 1934, the Court unanimously held that a student at a state-supported university could not refuse to attend required courses that offended his/her religious scruples (in this instance, ROTC training).

Justice Butler, speaking for the Court, said in his dicta,

The fact that [students] are able to pay their way in this University but not in any other institution in California is without significance . . . California has not drafted or called them to attend the University. [p.262]

Attendance was voluntary, not mandatory; and exemptions were a privilege, not a right.

Butler also said that religious exemption from military service was not a constitutional right guaranteed by the Free Exercise Clause but a privilege granted by Congress. *[The Court has since reiterated that position, in Seeger (1965) and Welsh (1970).]*

[This anti-exemption decision based on voluntary attendance did not apply to public schools, of course. The Court made a distinction in Barnette (1943): Since school attendance was compulsory, conscientious objectors had a right to exemption from the flag salute.]

[There may be a conflict between the Court's position in Hamilton and its opinion in Torcaso (1961). In Torcaso, a state argued that nobody was compelled to hold public office; therefore, it was justified in imposing a religious test for notaries public. The state lost. The issue in both Hamilton and Torcaso was criteria of eligibility. Eligibility for public office was protected against a religious test, whereas eligibility for an education at a state college was not—at least in 1934. (See Bob Jones, 1974.)]

Cantwell

In Cantwell v Connecticut, 1940, the Court unanimously (no dissent being recorded) ruled unconstitutional the state's laws that permitted local authorities to prevent peaceful evangelism by Jehovah's Witnesses.

Referring to Reynolds (1897), the Court conceded that although freedom to believe was absolute, freedom to act religiously could be regulated "for the protection of society."[p.304] But the government could not apply regulation merely to suppress an unpopular idea.

The Court held that the state law violated the First Amendment's protection of free speech—and, incidentally, its religious guarantees. The law allowed a state official to refuse a license to solicit if he thought that the cause was not religious. He was thus in the position of arbitrarily deciding what constituted legitimate religious practice and of laying a "forbidden burden of censorship on the free exercise of religion."[p.307] *[See also Murdock (1943) and discussion under McCollum (1948).]*

The Court, speaking through Justice Roberts, stated specifically for the first time that the religion clauses of the First Amendment applied to the state governments:

> The fundamental concept of liberty embodied in that Amendment [the Fourteenth] embraces the liberties guaranteed by the First Amendment. The First Amendment declares that Congress shall make no law respecting the establishment of religion or prohibiting the free exercise thereof. The Fourteenth Amendment has rendered the legislatures of the states as incompetent as Congress to enact such laws.[p.303]

[Thus free exercise cases based on deprivation of liberty and of property could also be based on separation of church and state. After 150 years, the religion clauses of the federal Constitution became important also in establishment cases, the first of which was Everson (1947). Since then, the two First Amendment clauses have stimulated an almost feverish rise in litigation at all levels of jurisdiction.

[The situation addressed in Cantwell continues to arise in different forms. Quite recently, California and Pennsylvania courts have heard complaints against "disruptive" solicitation of alms in airports by members of the International Society for Krishna Consciousness.]

Barnette (and Gobitis)

In West Virginia State Board of Education v Barnette, 1943, the Court ruled (6-3) that a state could not force public school students (Jehovah's Witnesses here) to salute the flag if that practice violated their religious beliefs (that the flag is a "graven image," to which they would not "bow down").[p.629]

This decision dramatically reversed the position that the Court had taken (8-1) in Minersville (Pa.) School District v Gobitis (1940). At that time, the Court had declared the compulsory flag salute law not unconstitutional, on the grounds that the law was secular, that it applied to everyone equally, and that it was necessary for national unity and security. *[See discussion of reversals under Zorach, 1952.]*

Speaking for the Court in Barnette, Justice Jackson said that a compulsory flag salute and pledge violated the basic freedom that underlay all the guarantees of the First Amendment, only incidentally including freedom of religion:

> The very purpose of the Bill of Rights was to withdraw certain subjects from the vicissitudes of political controversy, to place them beyond the reach of majorities and officials and to establish them as legal principles to be applied by the courts. One's right to life, liberty, and property, to free speech, a free press, worship and assembly and other fundamental rights may not be submitted to vote; they depend on the outcome of no elections.[p.638]

[It has often been argued that since the majority of a community or a state or even the country favors a practice, the majority ought to have its way and not be dictated to or restricted by a minority. Jackson's words here furnish the Court's answer to that argument. The balance is between the minority's freedom from religion and the majority's freedom of religion in a state-sponsored situation. The issue also arose in the Schempp school devotions case (1963), where the Court said that the majority's "freedom" under such circumstances amounted to establishment.]

Jackson distinguished this case from the compulsory ROTC issue in Hamilton (1934) because university attendance is voluntary, while school attendance is compulsory.

The Court's opinion touched upon another important educational issue—that of indoctrination:

> Probably no deeper division of our people could proceed from any provocation than from finding it necessary to choose what doctrine and whose program public education officials shall compel youth to unite in embracing. . . . Those who begin coercive elimination of dissent soon find themselves exterminating dissenters. Compulsory unification of opinion achieves only the unanimity of the graveyard. . . . If there is any fixed star in our constitutional constellation, it is that no official, high or petty, can prescribe what shall be orthodox in politics, nationalism, religion, or other matters of opinion or force citizens to confess by word or act their faith therein. [pp.641,642]

[In actual practice, the theoretical "fixed star," an American nova, appears to be variable in intensity, because of baffling cloudiness or people's deliberate smokescreens. The problem becomes clear when one considers the specifics of moral education for the general welfare. See discussion under Welsh (1970).

[Just a year before Barnette, the Court upheld a statute, aimed at Jehovah's Witnesses, that imposed a license fee on the right to sell religious literature for evangelistic purposes. In 1943 the Court reversed that decision also, as part of its Murdock decision.

[As in Cantwell (1940) and Murdock, which had to do with licensing, both Barnette and Gobitis involved the issue of freedom of speech (or freedom from coercion to speak) more than religious liberty. Some people who are interested in both a maximum separation of church and state and the harmony or interdependence of the two religion clauses applaud this emphasis.

[They argue that if a practice is attacked as denying freedom of speech (and the press) rather than freedom of religion, then the Court need not consider whether the speech is religious. True governmental neutrality—among religions, between religion and irreligion, between church and state—would not label people or issues religiously. A free speech case avoids the question of an establishment of religion: Religion gets no special protection not given to other forms of expression. Nor need the Court balance the interests of the religion clauses, either against each other or against other public interests.

[Further, the emphasis on free speech and press avoids the necessity for officials (and the Court) to decide what is a legitimate religious practice deserving of protection and what is not—which was an issue in Cantwell. Another

...ding religious issues is to appeal to the Fourteenth Amendment's ...f equal protection of the law for a minority—that merely happens ...igious minority. Even after <u>Cantwell</u> applied the religion clauses ...s, the Court has on occasion continued its former practice of sub-...ing religious issues to those of free speech, equal protection, or other public interests.

[Opposing partisans object to the removal of religious issues. They say that many cases involve serious practical conflicts between the two religion clauses that can be resolved only by balancing the two interests and not by "evading" the issues. Furthermore, they feel that religion merits special, benevolent accommodation from the state.

[Until <u>Lemon</u> (1971), the Court favored accommodation in establishment cases, though not always in early free exercise cases, as we have seen. Accommodation in more recent free exercise cases may indicate the Court's shift to this position: In <u>Sherbert</u> (1963) the Court protected sabbatarians, and in <u>Yoder</u> (1972) it protected sectarians who were opposed to public high schools. <u>TWA</u> (1977), however, adds a question mark about the Court's accommodation to sabbatarians.

[The flag salute cases involved <u>Reynolds</u> (1878), which had said that the state could regulate religious actions that violated social duties or were subversive of good order. <u>Barnette</u> narrowed the <u>Reynolds</u> criteria for restraints on freedom of religion and freedom of speech, limiting legal restraints to acts that present a "clear and present danger" to the state or to the people, a phrase used in the <u>Cantwell</u> dicta. Later, the Court added another test: Does the state have a "compelling interest" (e.g., public safety, universal education) that requires a person to forgo his/her freedom to act; and cannot that interest be served in any other way? (See <u>Sherbert</u> and <u>Yoder</u>.)]

Everson

In <u>Everson</u> v <u>Board of Education</u> (of Ewing, N.J.), 1947, the Court (5-4) approved the use of public funds for bus transportation of nonprofit private (here, Catholic) school children or reimbursement to their parents for such bus fares.

The Court held that these practices primarily provided social welfare service (traffic safety) to pupils, and only incidentally aided the sectarian schools. Pupils were allowed to "ride in public buses to and from schools rather than run the risk of traffic," and the service was like police protection.[p.7] Thus, like the loan of secular textbooks in <u>Cochran</u> (1930), bus transportation did not violate the Fourteenth Amendment. It did not have a private purpose for which people were forced to pay without due process, but it served a public need that protected the rights of all taxpayers and children equally.

[A related question: What constitutes equal transportation? If the school district provides busing for public high school students within the district, must it provide busing to a neighboring district for students whose religious group does not have a sectarian high school within the district? Local practices vary.]

More important, the Court, speaking through Justice Black, said that such provision of transportation was also not a violation of the Establishment Clause of the First Amendment. *[This was the first case in which the Court applied the Establishment Clause to a state. Cantwell (1940) had extended both religion clauses to the states via the Fourteenth Amendment, but only free exercise was at issue in Cantwell, and that was subordinated to free speech.]* In Everson the Court ruled equally on both the Fourteenth Amendment's "deprivation of liberty" and the First Amendment's freedom from establishment of religion. It said that neither was abridged here.

The occasion called forth the first extended interpretation of the Establishment Clause. Although the decision rested on the child benefit criterion, the wall of separation theory was the basic doctrine, as it had been when the Court first considered the meaning of the Free Exercise Clause (Reynolds, 1878). The Court officially construed the Establishment Clause:

> [It] means at least this: Neither a state nor the Federal Government can set up a church. Neither can pass laws which aid one religion, aid all religions, or prefer one religion over another. Neither can force nor influence a person to go to or remain away from church against his will or force him to profess a belief or disbelief in any religion. No person can be punished for entertaining or professing religious beliefs or disbeliefs, for church attendance or non-attendance. No tax, in any amount, large or small, can be levied to support any religious activities or institutions, whatever they may be called, or whatever form they may adopt to teach or practice religion. Neither a state nor the Federal Government can, openly or secretly, participate in the affairs of any religious organizations or groups and vice versa. In the words of Jefferson, the Clause against establishment of religion by law was intended to erect a "wall of separation between church and State."[pp.15,16] . . . That wall must be kept high and impregnable. We could not approve the slightest breach. New Jersey has not breached it here.[p.18]

Black did say, however, that the New Jersey statute was on the verge of permissible practice.

[The Court has continued to define (and extend) that border, to include textbook loans (Allen, 1968) and tests and diagnostic services (Walter, 1977), and has favorably regarded lunches and health services.

[The Court's definition banned aid to all religions (over irreligion) as well as to one religion. Over the years, it has confirmed, in words and actions, its adherence to this principle, despite continuing protests.]

Black stated:

> That [First] Amendment requires the state to be neutral in its relations with groups of religious believers and non-believers; it does not require the state to be their adversary. State power is no more to be used so as to handicap religions than it is to favor them.[p.18]

[This criterion of "neutrality" appears in subsequent opinions. See discussion under Schempp (1963), where it is applied to the state's "relationship between man and religion," rather than between the state and groups of people, as here.

[The Court has relaxed its strict neutrality between religion and irreligion

in order to avoid the charge of hostility. It favors a "benevolent neutrali-ty," which allows the state to accommodate itself to religion: where the two religion clauses conflict with each other; where the benefit to religion is incidental, indirect, and remote; and/or where the state's involvement is not excessively entangling. (See Walz, 1970.)

[Rights guaranteed by the U.S. Constitution are, through the Fourteenth Amendment, binding on the states; but practices permitted by the Constitu-tion are not. For example, the states must allow alternatives to public schools (Pierce, 1925), but may refuse to provide transportation to nonpublic schools if the state constitution has a higher wall of separation (Luetkemeyer, 1974).

[Furthermore, even though the Supreme Court holds that a statute does not violate the U.S. Constitution, a state court may rule that it does violate an identical provision in the state constitution, by interpreting the language differently. (See discussion under Schempp.)

[In the fifteen years following Everson, eight state supreme courts ruled on busing. Seven said it violated the state's constitution. The issue was wheth-er the practice benefits religion at all, and in many instances states may not aid religion even indirectly. Wisconsin met this problem by amending its con-stitution in 1967, to exempt busing from that prohibition.

[In giving its opinion, the Court has often declared its doctrinal position before announcing its decision in the particular case at hand. The decision may then show that the present case falls within the practices that the doc-trine proscribes or protects, or else falls outside—as in Everson.

[Consistency between doctrine and decision is sometimes questioned. In Ev-erson, the Court's vehement adherence to strict separation and its subsequent ruling that bus transportation did not breach the wall of separation particu-larly irritated Justice Jackson. He opened his dissent with a reference to Ju-lia, in Byron's Don Juan, who "whispering 'I will ne'er consent,'—consented." [p.19]

[Fifteen years later, Justice Douglas, concurring in Engel (1962), said he then felt he had voted incorrectly with the majority in Everson, which was 5-4. And Justice Black, who wrote the Everson opinion, dissented in Allen (1968), which used Everson as a precedent to permit the loan of textbooks. In addi-tion, two justices who voted for the Allen decision had second thoughts about it seven years later, in Meek (1975).

[Two possibly conflicting principles of the Everson decision may have ac-counted for the close vote and the two lengthy dissents. The two principles have taken different directions. The "wall of separation" theory, specifically endorsed by the Court as an official interpretation or pronouncement, continued strong through McCollum, Zorach, McGowan, Torcaso, and Engel. But it has de-clined since 1962. The "child benefit" doctrine has grown in importance, not only in the Court but also in Congress (see Flast, 1968).

[Generally speaking, a new principle arises out of the limitations of the old one, from its inadequacy to deal reasonably with a new case. The Court makes a distinction and shows that the criterion is less than absolute and that

the new case falls outside the criterion. The Court does not necess[...]
pudiate the old criterion, but rather adapts it to the new situatior[...]

[Free exercise of religion is upheld, but religious practices ma[...]
ed. Religious practice may be limited, but only if it interferes with a com-
pelling interest of the state and there is no alternative. Sectarian schools
may not be supported, but their pupils may receive benefits. The pupils may
receive benefits at school, but only for their health, safety, and purely sec-
ular activities. Other benefits may be provided, but not on school premises.
Religious schools may not be aided—except incidentally. The wall of sep-
aration is not torn down, but made permeable. Government neutrality is not
abandoned, but made benevolent. Separation of church and state holds, but the
state may make accommodations. Accommodations may be indirect, remote, or in-
cidental, but not deeply entangling. In sum, universal and coherent princi-
ples are the ideal, so that decisions may be uniform and consistent; but such
principles are impossible to achieve because of changing and conflicting inter-
ests.]

McCollum

In (Vashti) McCollum v Board of Education (of Champaign, Ill.), 1948, the
Court (8-1) declared unconstitutional a released time religious education program in the public schools, even though non-participants went to the study
hall.

Speaking for the Court, Justice Black said that the released time practice,
unlike transportation in Everson (1947), did not have a separable secular purpose. Instead, it was

> beyond all question a utilization of the tax-established and tax-support-
> ed public school system to aid religious groups to spread their faith.
> [p.210] . . . Here not only are the State's tax-supported public school
> buildings used for the dissemination of religious doctrines. The State
> also affords sectarian groups an invaluable aid in that it helps to pro-
> vide pupils for their religious classes through use of the State's com-
> pulsory public machinery. This is not separation of Church and State.
> [p.212]

Citing Everson, the Court specifically rejected the argument that "the First
Amendment was intended to forbid only government preference of one religion
over another, but not an impartial assistance to all religions": The Establishment Clause read, "an establishment of religion," not "a religion" and not
"churches." "Separation of church and state" was a slogan for separation of
religion and state. Everson had said that neither a state nor the federal government could "aid one religion, aid all religions, or prefer one religion over
another."

The Court also rejected the argument that the released time program did not
violate the religion clauses since participation was voluntary. Coercion,
Black said, was evidence of violation of the Free Exercise Clause, but aid to
religion violated the Establishment Clause regardless of coercion. *[See Engel,*
1962.] And the McCollum youngster testified that he had suffered harassment
for his nonconformity.

Black quoted the Everson dicta about the wall of separation, noting that the

Collum ruling did not "manifest a governmental hostility to religion." Instead, he explained,

> the First Amendment rests upon the premise that both religion and government can best work to achieve their lofty aims if each is left free from the other within its respective sphere.[p.212]

[Thirty years after McCollum, accommodationists have not given up. In a current suit, a Michigan school district is defending voluntary religious classes during school hours on school property, conducted by a Bible mission.]

Those interested in the field of teaching about religion and/or studying the Bible in public school call attention to Justice Jackson's concurring opinion [i.e., _voting with the majority but for different reasons_]:

> Certainly a course in English literature that omitted the Bible and other powerful uses of our mother tongue for religious ends would be pretty barren. And I should suppose it is a proper, if not indispensable, part of preparation for a worldly life to know the roles that religion and religions have played in the tragic story of mankind. The fact is that, for good or for ill, nearly everything in our culture worth transmitting, everything which gives meaning to life, is saturated with religious influences . . . One can hardly respect a system of education that would leave the student wholly ignorant of the currents of religious thought that move the world society for a part in which he is being prepared. [p.236]

[This case also raises a non-educational church-state issue. If public property (here, schools) may not be used for state-sponsored religious purposes, may tax-supported public parks be so used—for a cross (see Lowe, 1969) or for Christmas nativity scenes? It is not unconstitutional for religious groups to use school buildings after hours and parks without governmental involvement as a sponsor. In Poulos (1953), the Court ruled that a municipality might constitutionally insist that religious groups not be denied a license for religious services in a public park: licensing was legal, but not the religious test for a license—as in Cantwell (1940).

[A footnote to McCollum is a recent decision by the New Jersey supreme court that Transcendental Meditation is a religious activity and should not be taught in public schools.]

Doremus

In Doremus v Board of Education (of Hawthorne, N.J.), 1952, the Court denied certiorari (refused to hear the case) for lack of jurisdiction. The state supreme court had ruled that the reading of Bible verses without comment and with permission for dissenters to absent themselves did not violate the Establishment Clause of the federal Constitution. The effect of the Supreme Court's non-ruling was to let that decision stand.

The state court had said that the small amount of time and expense involved did not constitute establishment of religion, that the Old Testament and the Lord's prayer were nonsectarian, and that theism and the Judeo-Christian heritage had formed and now suffused the American character and culture.

In denying the appeal, Justice Jackson spoke for the Cour[t]
three related reasons. First, the student who claimed inju[r]
Second, the remaining adults in the case, as mere taxpayers
sue in the U.S. Supreme Court without "requisite financial
And third, the stipulated facts, accepted by both sides wi[th]
without lower court trial) showed insufficient injury beca[use]
compelled to accept, respond to, or even listen to the Bi[ble]

[The case received wide publicity and was claimed as a victory at [loc]al level for champions of Bible reading in the schools. They saw it as a step back by the Court from the extreme separationism of the McCollum released time decision (a hope that was soon bolstered by the sanctioning of dismissed time in Zorach, 1952). But this was an instance of reading too much into a denial of certiorari. In Engel (1962) and Schempp (1963), the Court contradicted the position taken by the New Jersey supreme court in Doremus.

[The Court often gives no reason when it dismisses an appeal. On one occasion it did say that it might refuse a case if the federal question it raised "is wholly formal, is so absolutely devoid of merit as to be frivolous, or has been so explicitly foreclosed by a decision of this court as to leave no room for real controversy." The Court may have still other reasons, particularly a lack of jurisdiction, as in Doremus.

[Such a "non-ruling" has the effect of upholding the lower court's decision. As we have seen in Doremus, however, it is unsafe to infer that the Court's denial of certiorari means approval of that decision. Another example of misleading inference in the field of education and religion: In Horace Mann League (1966), the Court denied a hearing to an appeal from a ruling which said that a state (Maryland) could not give grants of any kind to church-affiliated colleges. The Court reversed the effect of its non-ruling, in Tilton (1971) and in Roemer (1976). Nevertheless, lawyers and judges often cite a lower court's decision and a Supreme Court non-ruling on it to support an argument or an opinion in a case involving the federal Constitution.

[The Court has refused to hear, and thereby, at least in effect, upheld many lower federal or state court decisions that declared certain forms of parochi-aid illegal. Examples from Vermont: tuition grants by school districts that do not have public high schools, for their students to attend nearby Catholic high schools; municipal support for a local parochial school and calling it a public school, where the town could not afford its own school.]

Zorach

In Zorach v Clauson, 1952, the Court upheld (6-3) a New York City dismissed time religious education program during school hours at religious centers, with non-participants required to remain in school.

[Although the program was referred to as both released time and dismissed time, it is useful to distinguish arbitrarily between the two terms: released time, religious instruction within the school building; dismissed time, outside it.]

The Court, speaking through Justice Douglas, said that this case differed from McCollum (1948) in that although the school distributed parent consent

ok attendance, and adjusted its schedule to accommodate the program,
s not the same deep involvement of the public school authorities in the
ous education program. This was no different, said Douglas, from excus-
pupils for religious observances at their places of worship.

["Degree of involvement," cited here as a criterion, becomes more important
later, beginning with the question of church property taxes in Walz (1970).
The use of school premises was the crucial factor in determining excessive involvement in McCollum and Zorach. The same test appeared again in Walter
(1977), which dealt with on-the-premises diagnostic, remedial, and counseling
services; but in that case the question of who furnished the service was
equally important.

[There may have been other considerations influencing the Court's departure
from McCollum. That decision had been widely attacked by most of the organized
church groups and in many legal journals. In addition, two members of the Mc-
Collum majority had since left. Also, the country was now in the grip of a Mc-
Carthyite hysteria about "atheistic communism" in America.

[If these extra-legal factors did partially explain the rather narrow distinction (critics called it inconsistency) between McCollum and Zorach, it
would not have been unique in the history of the Court. One consideration in
the Barnette (1943) flag salute decision may very well have been the cruel per-
secution of Jehovah's Witnesses that followed upon the Gobitis (1940) ruling.
In 1940, war was imminent and the atmosphere was charged; by 1943, the allies
were winning and patriotic anxiety about the flag salute was more relaxed. The
humorist had the cynical Mr. Dooley say that the Supreme Court followed the
election returns.

[Scholars who see a discrepancy between the Zorach and McCollum decisions
differ as to its significance: Which one was the aberration in the proper interpretation of the religion clauses? Generally, these scholarly differences
arise out of a commitment to either separationism or accommodationism.]

The Court reiterated its adherence to the separation of church and state
"within the scope" of the First Amendment, but indicated that the scope was
limited and did not include dismissed time religious instruction. At least,
it permitted the state to make accommodations for religion. In fact, the Court
for the first time officially questioned the dimensions and impermeability of
the wall of separation:

> The First Amendment, however, does not say that in every and all respects
> there shall be a separation of Church and State. . . . Otherwise, the
> state and religion would be aliens to each other—hostile, suspicious,
> even unfriendly. [p.312]

If separation were absolute, Douglas argued, churches could not be required
to pay any taxes and municipalities could not render police or fire protection
to religious groups. Also forbidden would be prayers in legislative halls, appeals to the Almighty in Presidential messages, proclamations of Thanksgiving
Day as a holiday, and taking an oath for court testimony. He echoed the senti-
ments expressed in the Sunday observance case of Holy Trinity (1892). There,
Justice Brewer had advocated a friendly attitude toward religion (which in his
terms, however, was synonymous with Christianity: "This is a Christian nation"). [p.471] Douglas interpreted the term somewhat more broadly:

We are a religious people whose institutions presuppose a Supreme Being
. . . When the state encourages religious instruction or cooperates by
adjusting the schedule of public events to sectarian needs, it follows
the best of our traditions. For it then respects the religious nature of
our people and accommodates the public service to their spiritual needs.
To hold that it may not would be to find in the Constitution a requirement that the government show a callous indifference to religious groups.
That would be preferring those who believe in no religion over those who
do believe . . . [S]eparation of Church and State [does not] mean that
public institutions can make no adjustments of their schedules to accommodate the religious needs of the people. We cannot read into the Bill
of Rights such a philosophy of hostility to religion. [pp.313ff.]

[This position has possible implications for the school calendar: adjusting
schedules for religious holidays, offering educational activities on Saturday
or Sunday, offering afternoon or evening enrichment or make-up activities that
conflict with the hours of religious schools—in communities where the affected
minority is sizable.

[Some people misunderstood Douglas's remarks to be a denial of the "wall"
metaphor that had been championed in the Everson busing case (1947). But he
later explained that the "accommodation" theory was offered only as an amelio-
ration of absolute separation. (See Torcaso, 1961, and McGowan, 1962; see
also discussion under Everson.) The line between accommodation and aid to religion is delicate, especially when the two religion clauses clash. Sometimes
a too rigid enforcement of the Establishment Clause would inhibit free exercise, as would be true if the army refused to provide chaplains or if firemen
let a church building burn down rather than violate separation of church and
state.

[Separationists have recently claimed in lower courts that the Zorach decision was based on a now outdated criterion and should be reviewed: Today, a
practice has to meet the requirement of a secular purpose to be constitutional.
Nevertheless, in 1976 the Court rejected without comment an appeal from a federal district court's approval of a dismissed time religious education program
in Harrisonburg, Va. In that instance, the classes were held in trailers near
the school and the regular teachers escorted their pupils to the trailer door
and then back again afterwards. (A current suit in Utah challenges the granting of academic credits to public secondary school students for attendance at
dismissed time religious education classes.)

[Incidentally, Douglas used the words "sectarian" and "religious" almost
synonymously here, ignoring the possibility of a personal, subjective "religion." This is relevant to the discussion under Welsh (1970). Furthermore,
his definition seems to limit the religiousness of the American people and its
institutions to theistic beliefs. That may have been true of the founders, but
then his argument about present-day institutions would have less force in the
case at hand: Some of our religions do not presuppose a Supreme Being.]

Burstyn

In Joseph Burstyn, Inc. v Wilson, 1952, the Court unanimously held unconstitutional a New York statute that authorized the state department of education
to refuse to permit the showing of motion picture films which its censors found

immoral or sacrilegious.

The Court, speaking through Justice Clark, said,

> The state has no legitimate interest in protecting any or all religions from views distasteful to them which is sufficient to justify prior constraints upon the expression of these views. It is not the business of government in our nation to suppress real or imagined attacks upon a religious doctrine.[p.565]

If censorship of sacrilegious films were permitted, he added, it would in reality require the censor to determine which religious sensibilities to protect. Delimiting religion tends toward establishment of orthodoxy.

[This decision, which brought films under freedom of speech and press for the first time, has at least two implications for what is taught in public schools and how it is taught. First, religious groups, like others, often bring pressure on schools to eliminate teaching materials and methods that the groups consider offensive. Most attacks on "obscene" textbooks have their origin in or are combined with religious sanctions—as in a recent widely publicized West Virginia crusade against "immoral and Godless books."

[Second, determining what is religion, which the Court was eager to avoid, is related to the twin problems of teaching about religion and fostering moral and spiritual values. (See discussion under Welsh, 1970.)

[Incidentally, some states still have statutes forbidding blasphemy against God, Jesus Christ, and/or the Bible. The laws have not been used, or challenged, for decades.]

Gideons

In Gideons International v Tudor, 1954, the Court, without explanation, denied certiorari to an appeal from a New Jersey supreme court decision that held unconstitutional Bible distribution through public schools.

[Other state supreme courts have since ruled similarly, some forbidding distribution on school grounds as well; but no case has reached the federal Supreme Court, although the practice continues in many school districts.]

McGowan

In McGowan v Maryland, 1961, the Court upheld (8-1) state "blue laws" that made it a crime to conduct business activities on Sunday.

The Court rejected the charge that the laws violated the religion clauses. The original intent of Sunday closing laws, said the Court, may have been religious, to force people to observe the Lord's day and attend church. But the purpose and effect had, over the years, become secular—for social welfare. The law designated a public day of rest, which particularly benefited laborers and shopkeepers. Furthermore, Maryland permitted the sale of alcoholic beverages and the operation of gambling machines on Sunday, surely not an advancement of religion. As with school busing in Everson (1947), benefits to religion were only remote and incidental, the Court felt.

Chief Justice Warren, speaking for the Court, said that if such state law elsewhere were still primarily religious in intent, they would be unconstitutional. *[This would seem to contradict the effect of the Holy Trinity (1892) ruling, which upheld Christian Sunday observance laws.]* Since their purpose in Maryland was secular (although local ordinances referred to Sunday as the Lord's Day), the laws were not unconstitutional in that state. States with constitutionally acceptable Sunday closing laws, Warren advised, were permitted, but not compelled, to grant exemptions to Christian sabbatarians and Orthodox Jews. *[Most states have done so.]*

The Court used the same reasoning in three other Massachusetts and Pennsylvania blue law cases that it decided on the same day: Two Guys from Harrison-Allentown, Inc. v McGinley; Braunfeld v Brown; and Gallagher v Crown Kosher Super Market. McGowan and Two Guys were simple supermarket cases and were decided 8-1.

Braunfeld and Crown involved Orthodox Judaism, and the Court split 6-3. All four litigants charged establishment of religion, but Orthodox Jews (and sabbatarian allies) added a free exercise charge. They complained that their freedom to practice their religion (which required Saturday closing) was inhibited by the financial penalty of losing a day's income. The Court rejected the argument. *[The effect of the Court's attitude toward such people was somewhat softened in Sherbert (1963), a sabbatarian employment compensation case.]*

Warren also refuted the argument that the Establishment Clause referred only to a specific kind of eighteenth century establishmentarianism rather than to a broad separation. If so, he said, the authors would have so worded the clause.

> But the First Amendment, in its final form, did not simply bar a congressional enactment establishing a church; it forbade all laws respecting an establishment of religion. Thus, the Court has given the Amendment a "broad interpretation." [original emphasis] [pp.441,442]

[The Court expanded this distinction in the Lemon opinion (1971): "Respecting" an establishment means "a step that could lead to" establishment. [p.612] The word "respecting" also protected the original states against federal laws that might interfere with their existing established religions, but that consideration has become irrelevant.]

In his dissent, Justice Douglas took the occasion to clarify and soften the language of the Zorach dismissed time decision (1952), which he had written:

> The Puritan influence helped shape our constitutional law and our common law . . . For these reasons we stated in Zorach v Clauson . . . "We are a religious people whose institutions presuppose a Supreme Being." But those who fashioned the First Amendment decided that if and when God is to be served, His service will not be motivated by coercive measures of government. . . . [I]f a religious leaven is to be worked into the affairs of our people, it is to be done by individuals and groups, not by the government. [p.563]

[The McGowan and associated rulings upholding Sunday laws, even though the laws were construed as nonreligious, have possible implications for the school calendar; e.g., scheduling activities for Saturday, which is the sabbath for several sects.]

Watkins, 1961, the Court unanimously declared unconstitutional
  ~ that required a profession of belief in the existence of God be-
 ~ould hold public office.

~ne Court thus extended to state officers the U.S. Constitution's ban on re-
~igious tests for federal office (Article VI, Section 3). The decision rested
on the "wall of separation." Speaking for the Court, Justice Black specifically rejected the argument that Douglas's dicta in Zorach (1952), which weakened
the wall's solidity, gave states the right to restore this kind of religious
involvement. He also said that it was unconstitutional to

> impose requirements that aid all religions as opposed to nonbelievers [or
> that] aid those religions based on belief in the existence of God as
> against those religions founded on different beliefs.[p.495]

Mr. Torcaso was a member of the American Humanist Association. In a footnote to the passage just cited, the Court said,

> Among religions in this country which do not teach what would generally
> be considered a belief in the existence of God are Buddhism, Taoism, Eth-
> ical Culture, Secular Humanism, and others.[p.495,n.11]

*[Of those named, secular humanism further varies from conventional "reli-
gions" in that it is not an organized sect: one need not belong to the association. Many people point to this footnote as a milestone in the change of the
Court's working definition of religion. The implications for teaching about
religion and for fostering moral and spiritual values in public schools may be
important (see discussion under Welsh, 1970).*

*[Incidentally, in April, 1978, the Court ruled unconstitutional a Tennessee
law that prohibited clergymen from serving in the legislature—a religious test
that the state had justified in the name of separation of church and state.]*

Engel

In Engel v Vitale, 1962, the Court (6-1) held unconstitutional the recita-
tion of a prayer composed by a group of clergymen for the New York Board of Regents as part of its program of "moral and spiritual training in the schools."

The opening clause of the prayer read, "Almighty God, we acknowledge our de-
pendence upon Thee." *[A mouthful for little children.]* Despite a provision to
excuse non-participants, the practice was a religious activity that breached
the wall of separation between church and state, said the Court; and it was
reminiscent of the British government's sponsorship of the Book of Common Prayer. Speaking for the Court, Justice Black said that the Establishment Clause

> must at least mean that in this country it is no part of the business of
> government to compose official prayers for any group of the American peo-
> ple to recite as a part of a religious program carried on by government.
> [p.425]

He said that the practice was closer to McCollum (1948) than to Zorach
(1952)—the released time and dismissed time cases respectively—because it
took place on school premises:

The Establishment Clause, unlike the Free Exercise Clause, does not depend on any showing of direct governmental compulsion . . . When the power, prestige, and financial support of government is [sic] placed behind a particular religious belief, the indirect coercive pressure upon religious minorities to conform to the prevailing officially approved religion is plain. [pp.430,431]

[As a matter of fact, direct governmental compulsion may not be necessary to act as coercion in free exercise violations, either. The same kind of governmental and social pressure that forces minorities to conform to majority religious practices may cause them to forgo their own nonconforming practices, especially among children. (See McCollum.)]

The Court said that the First Amendment applied to religion, not only to religions:

The fact that the prayer may be denominationally neutral . . . can [not] serve to free it from the limitations of the Establishment Clause. [p.430]

As it had in McCollum, the Court deliberately rejected the argument that its holding would "indicate hostility toward religion or toward prayer." [p.434] It also made clear, in a footnote, that the decision should not be construed as discouraging school children from expressing

love for our country by reciting historical documents such as the Declaration of Independence, which contain references to the Deity, or by singing officially espoused anthems which include the composer's professions of faith in a Supreme Being, or . . . [the] many manifestations in our public life of belief in God. Such patriotic or ceremonial occasions bear no true resemblance to . . . religious exercise. [p.435,n.21]

[The state expects schools to foster love of country; the Court considered any benefits to religion incidental. Presumably, the footnote left religious (or irreligious) objectors the right not to participate in such patriotic exercises that do mention God, as in the Barnette (1943) flag salute case. Note that by distinguishing between a patriotic and a religious exercise, the Court came close to defining the limits of what does and does not constitute religious practice. The Court has always shied away from becoming too specific, because such a definition of religion would tend to establish a sort of orthodoxy in matters of religious practice. (See Burstyn, 1952.)]

In answer to the argument that the Regents prayer was harmless, Black quoted with approval from Madison's "Remonstrance": "It is proper to take alarm at the first experiment on our liberties."

[In the course of a concurring opinion, Justice Douglas said he had voted incorrectly with the majority when it sanctioned busing in Everson (1947), which was decided 5-4. He now felt that many government-supported practices were unconstitutional, including chaplains in Congress and in military academies. [p.443]

[Engel was the first morning devotions case accepted by the Court. Its decision brought loud criticism from religious groups, partly because Doremus (1952) had led them to expect the Court to uphold "nonsectarian" (i.e., interdenominational theist) devotions. One result of the criticism was the justices'

detailed explanations in their Schempp opinions, the following year.]

Schempp/Murray

In <u>Abington School District</u> v <u>Schempp</u>, 1963—combining this Pennsylvania case with one from Maryland, <u>Murray</u> (Madalyn Murray, now O'Hair, and son) v <u>Curlett</u>—the Court held (8-1) that devotional reading of the Bible and school sponsored prayer (the Lord's Prayer, in both cases) were violations of the Establishment Clause of the First Amendment.

The decision rested on a newly articulated interpretation of the clause: The Court, speaking through Justice Clark, said,

> The test may be stated as follows: what are the purpose and the primary effect of the enactment? If either is the advancement or inhibition of religion, then the enactment exceeds the scope of legislative power as circumscribed by the Constitution. That is to say that to withstand the strictures of the Establishment Clause there must be a secular legislative purpose and a primary effect that neither advances nor inhibits religion. [p.222]

[These criteria—secular purpose and neutral primary effect—grew out of the "child benefit" doctrine of <u>Everson</u> (1947, busing), the breach in the "wall of separation" made in <u>Zorach</u> (1952, dismissed time), and the "purpose and effect" grounds of <u>McGowan</u> (1961, Sunday blue laws).]

The <u>Schempp</u> opinions ran to 115 pages. Justices comprehensively reviewed almost every argument on both sides, as well as nearly the entire history of the religion clauses, their background and their interpretation. The Court's official opinion rejected once again several contentions of proponents (not necessarily in the following order):

First, it was argued that there was no establishment of religion because participation was voluntary. (Sometimes, exempted students were sent to stand in the hall outside the homeroom, missing possible school announcements.) Clark replied that the practice supported religion, he referred to former opinions about indirect coercion upon non-participating children, and he reiterated a Court principle:

> A violation of the Free Exercise Clause is predicated on coercion while the Establishment Clause violation need not be so attended. [p.223]

Second, proponents said that the Bible reading was not a religious exercise but was secular in intent, seeking to promote moral values. (One attorney suggested that its purpose and effect were to calm down the pupils for their ensuing classes.) In response, the Court pointed to the "place of the Bible as an instrument of religion" and to

> the State's recognition of the pervading religious character of the ceremony . . . from the rule's specific permission of the alternative use of the Catholic Douay version as well as . . . permitting nonattendance at the exercises. [p.224]

Pennsylvania also permitted the Revised Standard and the Jewish Publication Society versions as alternatives.

Third, it was claimed that the time and money devoted to the exercises were insignificant and did not "establish" a church. The Court answered,

> It is no defense to urge that the religious practices here may be relatively minor encroachments on the First Amendment. The breach of neutrality that is today a trickling stream may all too soon become a raging torrent and, in the words of Madison, "it is proper to take alarm at the first experiment on our liberties."[p.225]

[The Court has expressed two seemingly polar opinions on this point. In Lemon (1971), the sectarian school teacher salary case, the Court defined "respecting establishment" to mean any tendency toward establishment. In Walz (1970), the church property tax case, the Court declared a "minor encroachment" to be harmless. Of course, the circumstances were different.]

Fourth, proponents contended that forbidding these practices interfered with the majority's free exercise of religion. *[See discussion under Barnette, 1943.]* The Court replied that the Free Exercise Clause

> has never meant that a majority could use the machinery of the State to practice its beliefs.[p.226]

Fifth, it was asserted that prohibiting these practices showed hostility toward religion, established a "religion of secularism" in the schools, and drove the Bible and religion from the schools. Clark pointed to the many previous opinions that had acknowledged the importance of religion in our society and went still further:

> It might well be said that one's education is not complete without a study of comparative religion or of the history of religion and its relation to the advancement of civilization. It certainly may be said that the Bible is worthy of study for its literary and historic qualities. Nothing we have said here indicates that such study of the Bible or of religion, when presented objectively as part of a secular program of education, may not be effected consistently with the First Amendment. [p.225]

[Clearly, to exclude religion and the Bible from academic study is not to be neutral. Given their place in our culture, their exclusion would imply an attack on their importance. The Schempp opinion does not go so far as to mandate academic study of religion and the Bible in order to overcome such an implied bias, but it does permit such study and even urges it. (In 1977, plaintiff taxpayers voluntarily dropped their suit which charged that Missouri public schools were teaching the religion of secular humanism.)

[In keeping with Schempp, students in public schools and colleges may study the Bible either as a religious and historic document or as a piece of literary art. They may read it in relation to the ancient civilizations in which it was produced or in relation to subsequent cultures (including our own) upon which it has had an influence—social, political, religious, literary, or artistic. An "objective" approach or attitude toward the academic study of religion, in a program of education that has a secular purpose and atmosphere is permissible in a state supported school or college. (See also Calvary Bible, 1968, and Tilton, 1971, both college cases.)]

Although not specifically questioned, Clark repeated at the outset two more of the Court's positions. First, the Establishment Clause, through the Fourteenth Amendment, applies to the states as well as to Congress, even though the clause begins, "Congress shall make no law." Second, the Establishment Clause forbids preference of religion over irreligion as well as one sect over others, as the Court had said in <u>Everson</u> (1947) and <u>McCollum</u> (1948). He reaffirmed this latter doctrine in these words:

> In the relationship between man and religion, the State is firmly committed to a position of neutrality.[p.226]

For Clark, neutrality meant that the Establishment and Free Exercise Clauses respectively prohibit the state from advancing or inhibiting religious belief and practice.

[In his lengthy concurring opinion, Justice Brennan stressed that when the two interests conflicted, strict neutrality might show hostility toward religion: for example, as when the army might refuse to provide chaplains. Neutrality in such cases should show benevolence toward religion.]

Those interested in the issue of teaching about religion and/or studying the Bible in public school also take note of two concurring opinions. Justice Brennan said,

> The holding of the Court today plainly does not foreclose teaching <u>about</u> the Holy Scriptures or about the differences between religious sects in classes in literature or history. Indeed, whether or not the Bible is involved, it would be impossible to teach meaningfully many subjects in the social sciences or the humanities without some mention of religion. To what extent, and at what points in the curriculum, religious materials should be cited are matters which the courts ought to entrust very largely to the experienced officials who superintend our Nation's public schools. They are the experts in such matters, and we are not. [original emphasis][p.300]

Justice Goldberg took pains to combat the charge of hostility toward religion and then added a much-quoted distinction:

> Government must inevitably take cognizance of the existence of religion and, indeed, under certain circumstances the First Amendment may require that it do so. And it seems clear to me . . . that the Court would recognize the propriety of . . . teaching <u>about</u> religion, as distinguished from the teaching <u>of</u> religion, in the public schools. [original emphasis] [p.306]

[The dicta of Clark, Brennan, and Goldberg—coincidentally of different religions—about the academic study of the Bible and religion agree with Justice Jackson's concurring opinion in <u>McCollum</u>, the released time case.

[By the time of the <u>Schempp</u> case, nearly every state had constitutional guarantees of religious liberty (or separation of church and state) similar to the First Amendment's clauses. But similar laws are not always interpreted similarly by state supreme courts. Fourteen had ruled that Bible reading in public schools was legal, while eight had ruled it illegal.

[Generally, the point of difference was whether a court considered the Bible

a sectarian book. (See *Doremus*, 1952; see also discussion under *Everson*, 1947.) By 1963, thirteen states required Bible reading and another twenty-five permitted it.

[The *Schempp* ruling prohibiting prayers and devotional Bible reading in public schools was intended to settle the matter for all states uniformly. Local practices that clearly violate Supreme Court decisions are not always discontinued, however. The Court has no enforcement powers.

[Quite often, school boards simply ignore the law of the land until someone has the temerity to complain. Then too, there is always the hope of finding a slightly different practice or circumstance not prohibited by the ruling—or even the hope of a reversal of the decision. In any event, people who were outraged by the *Engel* and *Schempp* decisions continue today to repeat the original arguments and refuse to accept the Court's answers to each of the seven points discussed above.

[Large numbers of schools, especially in the south and the midwest, years after *Schempp*, still have prayers and devotional Bible reading as morning exercises. Other states and localities, having tried one method after another to get around the ruling, finally gave up. (See discussion under *Chamberlin*, 1964; the *Netcong* case, 1971; and the contrasting experiences in Alabama and Massachusetts, which follow here.)

[In an indignant reaction to the *Schempp* decision, the Alabama State Board of Education provided an alternative to the banned extra-curricular morning devotions. It incorporated devotional Bible reading into the curriculum as a course of study. School authorities ordered teachers to choose one or the other procedure on pain of dismissal. As late as February of 1971, the state superintendent of public instruction admitted that if the Alabama attorney general were asked to, and did, rule on the state law requiring these practices, they would probably be outlawed. But as yet the attorney general had not been officially asked nor had he ruled — this despite a current challenge by the Civil Liberties Union (which eventually caused the state supreme court to declare the practices unconstitutional).

[In contrast, after *Schempp* the Massachusetts commissioner of education sought and got a ruling from the state attorney general on the state's law requiring morning devotions. Thereupon the commissioner ordered all school districts to stop the practice. He forced compliance with the *Schempp* decision both by asking the attorney general to bring suit against districts continuing the illegal practices and by withholding state assistance funds from them. One school district, Leyden, challenged the state ruling in the courts, but went down with *Netcong*.

[Whether the difference between these two official state reactions represents a difference in attitude toward God or toward the law of the land is debatable. The chances are that most noncompliance by school administrators is a sign neither of religious fervor nor of defiance of the law. Research has found it generally to be due to the local establishments' ignorance of the law, their inertia, their desire to avoid conflict, their honest blindness to the issues and to violations, and/or the absence of an effective opposition to the practices.

[The practice of substituting a brief period of silent meditation for the devotional exercises is fairly widespread. It has been challenged, but the Supreme Court has not ruled on its constitutionality.]

Sherbert

In <u>Sherbert</u> v <u>Verner</u>, 1963, which the Court decided on the same day as <u>Schempp</u>, it held (7-2) that the religious freedom of a Seventh-day Adventist had been abridged by the denial of employment compensation to her because she refused to take a job requiring Saturday work.

The Court, speaking through Justice Brennan, laid down a criterion for governmental imposition of direct limitations and indirect burdens on the free exercise of religion. Limitations or burdens were justifiable only if the state could show a "compelling interest," not merely a reasonable legislative purpose —which had been the criterion until then.

[The new language, which is central to the compulsory education case of <u>Yoder</u> (1972), represents a great change since the rather general and vague language of <u>Reynolds</u> (1879), the bigamy case.

[The Court thus officially supported Brennan's position, put forth in his concurring opinion in <u>Schempp</u> and hinted at in his dissent in the <u>Braunfeld</u> (1961) Sunday closing case. "Strict and lofty" neutrality (<u>Everson</u>, 1947) and "wholesome" neutrality (Clark, in <u>Schempp</u>) might inhibit the free exercise of religion. The preferred course was a benevolent neutrality, an accommodationist concept that the Court has adopted in subsequent opinions.]

Chamberlin (and Wiest)

In <u>Chamberlin</u> v <u>Dade County</u> (Fla.), 1964—a case similar to <u>Schempp</u> but with a longer list of complaints against religious practices in the schools—the Court, refusing to rehear, summarily referred to <u>Schempp</u> and struck down the prayer and devotional Bible reading aspects of the case.

It did not, however, consider the other aspects: baccalaureate services, Christmas and Easter observances, a religious census among pupils, and a religious test for teachers ("Do you believe in God?"). A Florida trial court had held it unconstitutional to present Christmas nativity and Easter crucifixion and resurrection plays as part of religious observances in the schools. *[These issues became moot because by the time the case reached the Supreme Court, after much foot dragging by the Florida courts, the appellants had no children in the schools.]*

[As in many other states, school prayer and devotional Bible reading had continued in Florida despite <u>Schempp</u>. Authorities took the position that the ruling did not apply beyond Pennsylvania and Maryland; or, if it did, each state (or county, as here) could and should carry a separate fight to the Supreme Court until one or the other was exhausted. This ploy collapsed after <u>Chamberlin</u>'s summary invalidation. (See also <u>Netcong</u>, 1971.)

[In similar fashion, after <u>Nyquist</u> (1973) disallowed tuition reimbursements, tax credits, and purchase of services, the Court summarily struck down several similar parochiaid practices in other states. The same pattern of challenges

and automatic invalidations followed Meek (1975), which ruled out "auxiliary services." (See also Walter, 1977.)

[In Wiest v Mt. Lebanon School District, 1974, the Court denied certiorari to an appeal from a decision that upheld the right of public schools in Pennsylvania to include invocation and benediction prayers in their commencement programs—attendance at which was voluntary. Incidentally, baccalaureate services present a problem to some clergymen as well as to nonbelievers: certain churches forbid interdenominational religious ceremonies.

[91.5% of schools reported on in a 1976 survey were said to conduct holiday concerts with religious content, 45.5% staged religious pageants at Christmas and Easter, 56.5% used religious holiday decorations, and 52% provided for either released time or dismissed time religious instruction. Nevertheless, 55.9% of the respondents—educators, parents, and community leaders—"found the practices objectionable."]

Seeger

In U. S. v Seeger, 1965, (three cases combined into one) the Court unanimously granted religious conscientious objector (CO) exemptions from military service to three men who did not believe in a Supreme Being, despite the law's requirement of such a belief as a basis for one's objection.

Each objector elaborately stated his ultimate ethical and metaphysical beliefs and said that they were his religion, although he did not believe in a Supreme Being in the conventional sense. None claimed to be an atheist. One belonged to a Humanist Center.

Speaking for the Court, Justice Clark noted that the Universal Military Training and Service Act of 1948, Section 6(j), restricted CO exemption to

> persons who, by reason of their religious training and belief are conscientiously opposed to participation in war in any form. . . . "Religious training and belief," as used in the Act [means] "an individual's belief in a relation to a Supreme Being involving duties superior to those arising from any human relation but [not including] essentially political, sociological, or philosophical views or a merely personal moral code." [p.165]

The appellants charged that the CO section of the act violated the religion clauses of the First Amendment on two counts. First, it did not exempt nonreligious conscientious objectors and thus preferred religion over irreligion. Second, it discriminated between different forms of religious expression, preferring theistic religions.

Clark denied the charges and construed the act's exemptions as follows:

> The test of belief in a "relation to a Supreme Being" is whether a given belief that is sincere and meaningful occupies a place in the life of its possessor parallel to that filled by the orthodox belief in God of one who clearly qualifies for the exemption. [pp.165,166]

He quoted with approval Tillich's alternative definition of the word "God":

> Translate it and speak of the depths of your life, the source of your be-

ing, of your ultimate concern, of <u>what</u> <u>you</u> <u>take</u> <u>seriously</u> <u>without</u> <u>any</u>
<u>reservation</u>. [emphasis added by Clark][p.187]

*[Thus the Court reinterpreted the words "Supreme Being" out of its intended
meaning. But the Court went further and said that Congress had made a mistake
when it included those words in the act and hadn't really meant them.]*

Clark dismissed the 1948 act's specific definition of "religious training
and belief" as a confusing and unnecessary addition to the 1940 act, which had
carried no such definition. Quoting the Congressional committee report that
sponsored the 1948 bill, Clark said that the new act was merely "intended to
re-enact 'substantially the same provisions as were found' in the 1940 act."
[p.176] And the 1940 act had not mentioned a Supreme Being. He said that for
beliefs to function "religiously," they had only to be transcendent; any more
specific language only hindered rather than helped the legislative intent and
could therefore be ignored.

*[The earliest military service acts had defined "religious" to include mem-
bership in a sect. As broader perspectives emerged, later versions dropped
that requirement, along with belief in God or a Supreme Being. The 1948 act
reinstated this latter stipulation and caused such problems that the 1967 version again omitted it—partly because of the <u>Seeger</u> opinion.]*

Nevertheless, the Court did insist that in order to qualify for exemption,
one's "religion" had to object to all wars rather than only "unjust" wars. *[It
has been argued that this part of the act discriminates against some religious
beliefs—those that distinguish between just and unjust wars. (See <u>Gillette</u>,
1971.)]*

*[Although this case did not deal with an educational issue, it has implica-
tions for teaching about religion and for fostering moral and spiritual values
in public schools: It further broadens the definition of religion stated in
the <u>Torcaso</u> footnote (1961), until the line between religious and secular values begins to blur. (See <u>Welsh</u>, where the pacifist disclaimed religion completely, but received a religious exemption.)]*

<u>Flast</u>   (and <u>Frothingham</u>)

In <u>Flast</u> v <u>Cohen</u>, 1968, the Court declared (8-1) that taxpayers could challenge federal appropriations under certain circumstances—in this case, where
the Establishment Clause was involved.

This decision overturned the Court's former ruling, unanimously made in
<u>Frothingham</u> (1923), which held that only people directly affected could sue.
In <u>Flast</u>, taxpayers whose only interest was in the use of their tax money,
sought the right to bring suit. They wanted to challenge specific administrative acts (allocation of funds) under the Elementary and Secondary Education
Act (ESEA) of 1965. Their complaint would be that these instances of applying
the act (in accordance with its provisions) violated the Establishment Clause,
by aiding sectarian schools rather than children.

ESEA of 1965 provided for the loan of books and instructional materials for
"supplementary educational centers and services" for "educationally deprived
children." Such loans, centers, and services must a) specifically and neces-

sarily include sectarian school pupils; b) be under strictly public and strictly evenhanded control, with title to materials and equipment to remain with the public institutions; and c) be only for the purpose of relieving deprivation.

Congress based its inclusion of sectarian school pupils on the Supreme Court's "child benefit" doctrine. The act approved dual enrollment (or shared time) and other use of public education facilities by pupils of sectarian schools. Administrators also approved the use of sectarian schools as centers (which a state supreme court upheld in Hartington, 1972) and of sectarian school personnel as administrators of certain programs. It was these aspects of the law and of its allegedly biased administration that Flast wanted permission to challenge in court.

[One reason for the reversal of Frothingham may have been the Court's desire to respect the legislative intent of Congress. The Senate had passed the Judicial Bill of 1966, which would have given individuals standing in federal courts to challenge under the First Amendment certain statutes that made grants or loans to church-sponsored institutions. The bill had died in the House, largely because of the Frothingham precedent.

[As a result of Flast, administration of ESEA (and by implication the very language of the act itself) became subject to judicial review. So did administrative actions—and the substance—of statutes in some other areas of church-state contact that affect taxpayers only through use of their taxes. Among these has been a challenge to the Higher Education Facilities Act (HEFA) of 1963, which was decided in Tilton (1971).

[Two years after Hartington, the Court ruled on another ESEA-related case, in Barrera (1974). The issue was whether a state could refuse to give ESEA funds to sectarian schools because of state prohibitions. This was also quite different from Flast's central challenge to the constitutionality of the act, however. Such a basic attack has not yet (summer 1978) reached the Court. The matter long lay dormant, but interest revived as a result of Meek (1975), which denied state funds for "auxiliary services" on sectarian school premises.

[Congress augmented ESEA of 1965 with the Emergency School Assistance Act (ESAA) of 1972, which provided federal money for "minority" students and could be used for nonpublic school children falling within that category. Separationists have questioned the way this act also has been administered in sectarian schools.]

Allen

In Board of Education v Allen, 1968, the Court upheld (6-3) the constitutionality of a New York statute that required local boards to lend secular textbooks, approved by the public school authorities, to children in nonpublic secondary schools—including sectarian schools—viewing the loan as aid to parents and children rather than to schools.

The Court, speaking through Justice White, based the judgment on the "child benefit" theory of Everson (1947) and on the "neutral purpose and primary effect" of Schempp (1963). White acknowledged that "free books make it more likely that some children choose to attend a sectarian school"[p.244], but the indirect aid to the school was neither the purpose nor the primary effect of the statute. Like _Everson_, _Allen_ satisfied the _Schempp_ criteria.

[_This decision confirmed that of_ _Cochran_ _(1930), but moved the issue from the Fourteenth Amendment to the First Amendment. Yet, though the Supreme Court again declared that it was not a violation of the federal Constitution to lend textbooks to children in sectarian schools, several state supreme courts have since ruled that the practice violated state laws. Some said that the practice did benefit the schools primarily rather than the pupils, in contrast to the Supreme Court's opinion; other states forbade even indirect aid to sectarian schools. Challenges continue, both for and against the practice._

[_Furthermore, even in states where the_ _Allen_ _ruling is applicable, the Court's decision merely permits the state to offer this service, but does not mandate it. In fact, as of 1975, two such states specifically forbade it. This has also been true of bus transportation, which was permitted but not mandated in_ _Everson_. _(See also_ _Luetkemeyer_, _1974.) On the other hand, Congress (as opposed to the Court) may mandate such services as part of an enactment. The National School Lunch Act of 1946 required expenditure of funds to nonprofit (including sectarian) schools under pain of withholding federal funds to public schools. Two states refused the option._]

White said that though books, unlike buses, were used in teaching, "religious schools pursue two goals, religious instruction and secular education." [p.245] He rejected the notion that religion permeated all phases of the Catholic schools involved and said that the activities were separable.

[_This position conflicts with earlier official Catholic statements and later Court decisions, both of which held that such permeation was an essential factor of Catholic school education. White relied on testimony that secular instruction in Catholic schools was separable. He discounted evidence that textbooks purchased under the act were religiously biased. That was the fault of the administration, not of the act, he said. In any event, although White was joined in_ _Allen_ _by other justices, they did not support his doctrine of separability in_ _Lemon_ _(1971), the very next parochiaid case._

[_Some partisans took White's dicta to mean that the Court might look favorably upon grants to teachers of secular subjects in sectarian schools, as well as public funding for many other nonreligious school services, supplies, and equipment—even including pro rata tuition aids for the secular aspects of sectarian schooling. Pennsylvania, New York, Ohio, and other states promptly enacted such legislation. When the Court finally considered such statutes, however, in_ _Dicenso_ _(1971) and in both_ _Nyquist_ _and_ _Levitt_ _(1973), it struck them down. White was the only one who favored the practices._

[_In_ _Lemon_, _the Court invalidated state payment for "secular" teaching and took pains to say that it would not allow the_ _Everson_ _busing and_ _Allen_ _textbook loan decisions to be "used as a platform for yet further steps" to aid sectarian schools.[p.624] In_ _Walter_ _(1977), which allowed speech, hearing, and psychological testing on sectarian school premises, the Court may have taken a small step in that direction._

[_As used by White, the word "primary" in "purpose and primary effect" seemed to mean prior to other effects in time, not importance. In adopting criteria_ *for Lemon, however, the Court clearly intended the latter meaning: In its dicta, the Court spelled out the word "primary" to mean both "direct and immediate" and reinforced its intent by using the phrase "principal or primary effect."*

[Incidentally, Justices Brennan and Marshall said, in their Meek dicta (1975), that Allen, for which they had voted, might have been incorrectly decided and should be reconsidered. This added to the uncertainty caused by Douglas's second thoughts about Everson, which he expressed in Zorach (1952). Both the busing and the textbook decisions continued to be controversial—either as being too accommodationist or as justifying more accommodation.]

Epperson (and Brown)

In Epperson v Arkansas, 1968, the Court (without dissent) ruled that an Arkansas statute forbidding the teaching of evolution was invalid because it was an establishment of Christian orthodoxy.

Speaking for the Court, Justice Fortas said,

> There is and can be no doubt that the First Amendment does not permit the State to require that teaching and learning be tailored to the principles or prohibition of any religious sect or dogma.[p.106]

[Later opinions of the Court have referred to this decision because it based the test of establishment on whether a law has a clearly "secular legislative purpose."

[The 1927 Scopes "monkey trial" on this issue in Tennessee convicted Scopes and did not go to the Supreme Court. That state finally repealed its statute in 1947. Mississippi, last of the three states with such a law, did not repeal until 1972.

[Evolution continues to be a bone of contention in education. For several years the California Board of Education wrestled with an order to include creation by design—the biblical account being one possible version—as a mandatory alternative theory to be taught in its science or social science textbooks. In 1973 Tennessee lawmakers passed a "Genesis law," requiring that biology textbooks which included evolution theory should give equal emphasis to Creation. And in Brown v Houston (Tex.), 1974, the Court refused to review a decision that public school textbooks did not have to include the biblical theory of the creation of man as an alternative to evolution.]

Calvary Bible

In 1968 the Court refused to hear an appeal of, and in effect upheld, a ruling by the supreme court of the state of Washington in Calvary Bible Presbyterian Church v Board of Regents of the University of Washington that permitted the teaching of the Bible as a piece of literature.

The state supreme court had ruled that the tax-supported university's elective course, "English 390: The Bible as Literature," did not violate the First Amendment. It held that the use of critical, liberal scholarship did not necessarily imply human creative authorship and was not an attack on the traditional, conservative view that the Bible is the revealed word of God. The opinion read, in part:

> In the final analysis, plaintiffs contend: 1) that the Bible cannot be taught objectively as a course in literature, for the attempt to do so violates their personal beliefs (sectarian); hence the teaching is unconstitutional; 2) that the course is not taught objectively, but is slanted against the plaintiff's beliefs. . . . The [trial] court found that the course does not . . . advance any particular religious interest or theology. [original parentheses and emphasis] [436 P2d 194]

As for merely objective presentation of offensive views, the court replied that there could be no censorship against such a practice:

> Our constitution does not guarantee sectarian control of our educational system. [436 P2d 193]

[The Supreme Court's refusal to hear the case leaves the state decision standing. It is not binding on other states. (See discussion under Doremus, 1952.) In any event, one cannot argue conclusively from a decision concerning practices in a state-supported college to practices in public schools, as is evidenced by the distinction made in Tilton (1971). Nevertheless, Calvary Bible is often cited by people interested in the issue of teaching the Bible in public school literature classes because the state court closely examined the methods of such a practice. In the courts, however, the case has been cited only in relation to the standing of clergymen and religious groups to sue.]

Lowe

In Eugene Sand and Gravel v Lowe, 1970, the Court refused certiorari to an appeal from, and in effect upheld, the Oregon supreme court's decision that a privately financed cross, erected on public property (a 50-foot neon-lighted cross on a hill dominating Eugene, Oregon) violated the Establishment Clause.

[Such an issue might have relevance for the use of religious symbols and holiday decorations in public schools—provided that one takes into consideration the compulsory attendance of impressionable young children.

[Any inference is complicated, however, by the fact that the Court also denied certiorari in a similar case that was decided exactly opposite by the supreme court of Oklahoma in 1972 (Oklahoma City). The lower court felt that a 50-foot Latin cross on city grounds was "nonsectarian."

[Incidentally, Eugene's cross was not removed, despite the various court decisions. The electorate instead voted to designate it a war memorial, and early in 1977 the Oregon supreme court held (4-3) that the purpose was now secular and did not foster religion; therefore, it did not violate the state constitution. Six months later that year, the federal Supreme Court let the new decision stand by again refusing an appeal. (The failure to remove the cross when ordered by the court was consistent with the way it was erected—without a permit from the city council. Presented with a fait accompli, authorities conferred ex post facto legitimacy on this flouting of the law.)]

<u>Welsh</u>
(and other cases: <u>Girard</u>, <u>Watson</u>, <u>Davis</u>, <u>Ballard</u>, <u>Gillette</u>)

In <u>Welsh</u> v <u>U. S.</u>, 1970, the Court ruled (5-3) that deeply and sincerely held beliefs that are purely ethical or moral in both source and content (i.e., humanistic and subjective) are grounds for a religious conscientious objector (CO) military exemption, because they are held "with the strength of more traditional religious convictions."[p.340]

Section 6(j) of the Military Service Act of 1967 provided for the exemption of a person who,

> by reason of religious training and belief, is conscientiously opposed to participation in war in any form. As used in this subsection, the term "religious training and belief" does not include essentially political, sociological, or philosophical views, or a merely personal moral code.[p.332]

[This wording differs from the military service act of 1948 (reported in <u>Seeger</u>, 1965) mainly in eliminating the need for belief in a Supreme Being in order to qualify for a religious exemption.]

Welsh insisted, as Seeger and others had not, that his anti-war beliefs came from readings in history and sociology, not from religious training and belief. Despite the language of the act quoted above, the Court construed its words to allow Welsh a religious exemption.

Justice Black, speaking for the majority, specifically refused to reconsider whether religious exemptions in general, which exclude nonreligious people, violate the Establishment Clause by preferring religion over irreligion. He cited the Court's ruling in the 1918 <u>Selective</u> <u>Draft</u> <u>Law</u> <u>Cases</u>: Without giving a reason the Court had then held that religious exemptions (of clergymen) did not violate the Establishment Clause.

Justice Harlan concurred in the <u>Welsh</u> decision, but objected to Black's reasoning:

> It is a remarkable feat of judicial surgery to remove, as did <u>Seeger</u>, the theistic requirement [of the act]. The prevailing opinion today, however, in the name of interpreting the will of Congress, has performed a lobotomy.[p.398]

He felt that religious exemptions did violate the Establishment Clause, but he would rather "distort" the definition of religion than either deny CO exemptions of any kind or jeopardize the military system.

The Court also reiterated its fixed principle, stated in <u>Hamilton</u> (1934), the ROTC case, that CO exemptions were not a constitutional right under the Free Exercise Clause, but were a privilege granted by Congress in the military service laws.

*   *   *

[A major question raised by this case has to do with the definition of "religion." As construed by the Court in <u>Welsh</u>, the field of religion expands greatly (and that of irreligion narrows). One had not needed to belong to a sect or to believe in a Supreme Being. In the new, functional definition, a

person's "merely personal moral code," based on any kind of ultimate values, was his/her religion. The Court explained "Supreme Being" in _Seeger_ and "religious beliefs" in _Welsh_ in such a way that atheists who scorned religion might qualify for religious CO exemptions.

[The military service statutes have gradually departed from the traditional definition of religion. In harmony with the 1864 law, the Selective Service Draft Act of 1917 gave religious exemptions from combative service to members of

> any well-recognized religious sect or organization at present organized and existing and whose existing creed or principles forbid its members to participate in war in any form.

[The Selective Service Act of 1940 discarded the requirement of membership in a sect and substituted as a criterion a conscientious objection "by reason of religious training and belief." In practice, the assumption was that one's religion was theistic. In 1948, the new act legitimized practice; defined those words as involving belief in a Supreme Being; and eliminated purely philosophical, social, or political beliefs as permissible grounds. The "Supreme Being" clause caused so much trouble in _Seeger_ that the Court ignored it.

[By the 1967 version of the law, the definition of religion eliminated both sectarian membership and theistic belief. But it stopped short of allowing religious CO exemptions based on politics, sociology, philosophy, or on purely personal moral grounds. This final step the Court took in _Welsh_.]

In _Gillette_ v _U. S._, 1971, the Court struck down selective objection—to a particular war rather than to "war in any form." The Court again refused to rule on the constitutionality of religious exemptions as being "underinclusive" and advancing religion. Justice Marshall, speaking for the Court (8-1), defended the secularization of the definition of religion, saying that individual conscience was a more important ingredient than "sectarian affiliation or theological position." The use of a broad definition of religion to exempt Seeger and Welsh, he argued, was evidence that the Court acknowledged the "supremacy of conscience" and thereby showed that the Court was not preferring religion over irreligion:

> For thirty years the exempting provision has focused on individual conscientious beliefs . . . that are "religious" in nature. [p.454]

[Even more than in CO cases, the question of the definition of "religion" has been seriously debated in tax exemption cases, especially at the state and local levels. Nevertheless, education also has a stake in the issue.

[The roots of the problem for educators are as follows: Schools must foster moral values (_Pierce_, 1925), but may not foster religion (_Everson_, 1947). If the Court were to apply its _Welsh_ definition of religion consistently in all First Amendment cases, a public school teacher would face a dilemma. If the teacher believes in the moral values s/he teaches, and if purely moral beliefs—divorced from God and sect—constitute religious beliefs, then the teacher cannot foster moral values without fostering his/her religious beliefs.

[Furthermore, as Chief Justice Burger said in _Lemon_ (1971),

>What would appear to some to be essential to good citizenship might well
>to others border on or constitute instruction in religion.[p.619]

In fact, a Massachusetts parent sued his school district for teaching his
children the universal brotherhood of man—to which he would make important ex-
ceptions. (His grounds were that the concept, and the program, were sponsored
by Quakers and therefore were an unwarranted intrusion of religion into the
public schools. But the sectarian sponsorship is irrelevant to the problem at
hand.) The point is that every moral value can be challenged by some minority,
and minorities that once were philosophical become religious minorities under
the Welsh definition.

[As for which moral values should be taught in public schools, see the
Court's remarks in Barnette (1943), the flag salute case: "No official . . .
can prescribe what shall be orthodox in matters of opinion."[p.642]

[Some people have recently compounded the teacher's confusion by introduc-
ing the notion of the "religious dimension of education." This concept in-
cludes every aspect of values in schools: 1) the academic study of religion,
2) moral instruction, and 3) the values involved in the very process of education. Thus, one teaches even sports "religiously" (valuing self-reliance or
commitment to a group); the teacher cannot avoid religious indoctrination.

[Adding to the complexity is the Court's statement, in Zorach, the dismissed
time case (1952), that "we are a religious people whose institutions presuppose
a Supreme Being." The teacher must teach respect for law, love of country, and
commitment to democracy. To what extent does Zorach's dictum imply that our
national values are bound up with religiousness?

[As our country has grown more pluralistic in fact and in self-conscious-
ness, the traditional sect-oriented (and theistic) definition of religion has
seemed inadequate and in need of adjustment. Yet the newer purely value-cen-
tered (and subjective) definition has brought other problems.

[The Court's definition has undergone a process of broadening, secularizing,
and personalizing, particularly in CO cases. But the Court has not applied the
very broad definition—used in Welsh to construe a particular statute—to the
language of the First Amendment. The Court returned to a more traditional definition in Yoder (1972), which grants exemptions from compulsory school attendance, but only to members of long established sects.

[In a sense, the broader definition raises conflicts among some of the Constitution's purposes as set forth in the preamble. The preamble promises both
to provide for the common defense and to secure the blessings of [religious]
liberty. Welsh tries to balance those interests. But the preamble also promises to promote the general welfare (by fostering good citizenship through the
schools). Welsh's definition of religion makes it difficult for the teacher to
foster civic values without violating one of those liberties—freedom from religion.]

*   *   *

Here are some steps in the continuing history of the Court's struggle with
the definition of religion, limits on its practice, and its relation to moral
values.

Vidal v Girard, 1844, concerned an anti-clerical, though not anti-religious, bequest to a college. The unanimous Court, speaking through Justice Story, upheld the bequest since it was not inconsistent with the Christian religion, which "is a part of the common law of Pennsylvania."[p.198] The Court also declared its approval of the use of the New Testament for teaching moral truths in public schools because this is a "Christian country," as opposed to "judaism [sic] or Deism, or any other form of infidelity."[p.198]

Watson v Jones, 1872, dealt with the ownership of church property, disputed by pro- and anti-slavery factions of a Presbyterian church in Kentucky. The Court (3-2; others abstained or were absent) refused to define either religion in general or the particular religion involved in the dispute on the ground that to decide which side's views were correct would violate the Establishment Clause. The government would then be setting criteria by which to judge a sect's legitimacy. Not only would that establish government-approved religions, but it would also discriminate against the religious freedom of any sects or schismatics that did not meet the government's standards of belief and practice.

Justice Miller, speaking for the Court, removed the state from factional disputes and said that standards of legitimacy should come from within the sect:

> All who unite themselves to such a [religious] body do so with an implied consent to this [church] government. But it would be a vain consent and would lead to the total subversion of such religious bodies, if any one aggrieved by one of their decisions could appeal to the secular courts and have them reversed.[p.729]

[This decision established a precedent for the Court's policy in cases of intrachurch quarrels. The Court defers to the laws of the particular church before the schism. If hierarchical/episcopal or representative/presbyterian, the Court accepts the decision of the highest level of the polity; if congregational, that of the majority of the members. It has also insisted that no other branch of government may do otherwise. Recently the Court reaffirmed (7-2) its position in Serbian Orthodox Church (1976).]

The Court did, however, set some general limits on religion:

> In this country the full and free right to entertain any religious belief, to practice any religious principle, and to teach any religious doctrine which does not violate the laws of morality and property, and which does not infringe personal rights, is conceded to all.[p.728]

[The Court and the states have consistently upheld this position. Although there have been official statements about the higher obligation that people owe to God than to men and about the supremacy of conscience, duty to God or conscience has never been allowed to excuse violations mentioned here.]

In Reynolds (1878, discussed earlier), the Court specified one religious practice (and teaching) that violated the "laws of morality": polygamy.

In Davis v Beason, 1890, Justice Field, speaking for the Court, upheld government disenfranchisement of polygamous Mormons in the Territory of Utah. In so doing, he did define religion—from the traditional viewpoint:

> The term "religion" has reference to one's views of his relation to his

Creator, and to the obligations they impose of reverence for his being and character, and of obedience to his will.[p.342]

Field echoed Watson's limitation upon religion and said that free exercise was guaranteed

provided always the laws of society, designed to secure its peace and prosperity, and the morals of its people, are not interfered with.[p.342]

[This was one of a series of decisions restricting Mormons. Dissenters objected that the decision imposed something like a religious test on citizenshp, since the law against polygamy applied only to Mormons, and was so intended.]

In Cantwell (1940) the Court said that the state should not be allowed to decide what practices constitute religious exercise before granting permits to evangelize in public.

In U. S. v Ballard, 1944, the Court ruled (5-4) that the state could not prosecute the founders of an unconventional sect ("I Am") for the alleged "fraud" of promising miraculous cures and of claiming to have received their faith by revelation if they honestly believed in that revelation. Justice Douglas, speaking for the Court, said that verifiability of truth was not the question, and used these words from the Watson dicta:

The law knows no heresy, and is committed to the support of no dogma. [p.86]

He therefore avoided defining religion and took the position that the test of religion was whether or not it was sincerely believed to be religiously true, whether factually true or not.

[But determining sincerity of belief may be as difficult as defining religion, as Justice Jackson's dissent insisted. The Court replied that such a test was not unusual: judges and juries regularly evaluated the sincerity of witnesses. At any rate, this decision did not go so far as to sanction individual conscience rather than sectarian belief as the criterion for religion.]

In Zorach (1952), "religious" and "sectarian" are practically synonymous, with no room for humanistic or subjective conscience.

In Burstyn (1952), the Court, faced with determining what was sacrilegious, again deliberately refused to define religion.

[Thus far, the Court's implicit definition was generally conventional and traditional: belief in a Supreme Being, membership in a sect, and observance of certain practices of worship. Moral values, even in ultimate concerns, might be either religious or secular in source and content.]

In Torcaso (1961), the Court eliminated from "religion" the necessity of belief in a Creator and of belonging to a sect with cultic practices, but did not base a decision on that broader definition of religion. It was merely a footnote. Nevertheless, for the first time it included nontheistic religions with traditional religions.

In Schempp (1963), the Court distinguished between the religious purpose of traditional Bible reading exercises (which is unlawful) and the secular promotion of moral values (which is not). Furthermore, the Court said that schools might not use a religious means to achieve the secular end of inculcating moral and spiritual values—a point made earlier, in Engel (1962).

In Seeger (1965) the Court granted religious exemption from military service to people whose "religion" qualified within the Torcaso footnote. The Court acknowledged the "ever broadening understanding of the modern religious community"[p.180] and said that religious exemption covered an objector whose opposition to war was based on

> belief in and devotion to goodness and virtue for their own sakes, and a religious faith in a purely ethical creed.[p.166]

In fact, the Court clearly showed that the attempt by Congress to define religion theistically in the draft act clouded the issue and was best ignored. For the first time, the Court permitted functional equivalents to the conventional definition of religion.

In Welsh (1970), the Court said that personal moral codes and beliefs that were purely philosophical, social, and/or political in source and content were, for the purpose of construing the Military Service Act, religious. The sincerity of such beliefs, as in Ballard, was a crucial factor.

In Gillette (1971), also a draft law case, the Court admitted that it was using a secularized definition of religion. Nevertheless, Justice Marshall's dicta seemed to contradict the Court's commitment to equating religion with conscience by his frequent use of the expression "religion and conscience."

In Lemon (1971), the Court took notice of the difficulty of distinguishing between "what would appear to some to be essential to good citizenship" and "instruction in religion."

[Attempts to make good citizenship and religious morality synonymous, however apt theoretically, usually break down in the classroom and elsewhere over specific questions of practical moral decisions. God is often invoked on both sides of moral issues.]

In Yoder (1972), the Court exempted some children from compulsory school attendance because of their religious beliefs, which were legitimized in the Court's eyes by the fact that the children belonged to an "unworldly" sect.

[Yoder seems to indicate that the Court does not intend to apply the broad Welsh definition of religion in all instances. The Court specifically ruled out exemptions to people whose views were grounded in individual value systems. This may betoken either a return to the more conventional definition of religion or else a setting of limits to the application of the newer and broader definition.

[On the other hand, there may be a pragmatic consistency between the Welsh and Yoder decisions that transcends theoretical inconsistency. If the Court had used the narrower, traditional definition of religion in Welsh, then all exemptions and/or draft laws would have been in jeopardy. If it had used the broader, individualized definition in Yoder, then the public school system would have been threatened. Thus both decisions served the public interest. The state's interest in the "common defense" and the "general welfare" may have outweighed, for the Court, the hobgoblin of definitional consistency.]

Walz (and Murdock)

In Walz v Tax Commission (of New York), 1970, the Court ruled (7-1) that exemption from state taxes on church property used for religious purposes is not unconstitutional.

The Court had refused to hear cases appealing similar rulings by courts of Rhode Island in 1962 and Maryland in 1965. But Mr. Walz's challenge cited different authorities: President Madison, when retired, had said that such tax exemptions violated the First Amendment, which he had written. And some states showed their interest in and control over church property by limiting the amount a church could own. Nevertheless, Walz lost.

The Court, speaking through Chief Justice Burger, rejected the argument—urged not by New York City but by Catholic witnesses—that the Free Exercise Clause made exemption mandatory because a tax would inhibit religious freedom. Such exemptions, said the Court, were not a right but a privilege which the government granted.

On the charge of violating the Establishment Clause, the Court used three arguments. First, churches were only one of a class of institutions that received exemptions because they fostered the city's "moral and mental improvement." The criterion for exemption was not religion but public welfare, and to exclude churches from that class would show hostility to religion.

Second, tax exemptions, authorized by states and by Congress, had not in two hundred years worked toward establishment. *[This position is consistent with the McGowan interpretation of "respecting an establishment" as tending toward establishment. But the excuse that "it's always been done" has not saved other traditional practices as circumstances have changed.]*

Third, and most notable, was Burger's discussion of the degree of state involvement in religion: was it so great as to constitute excessive entanglement? Burger rephrased what the Court considered to be the framers' criteria for establishment: they were

> sponsorship, financial support, and active involvement of the sovereign in religious activity. [p.668]

Burger granted that some involvement could not be avoided if the government was to guarantee both nonestablishment and freedom of exercise. In Zorach (1952), the Court had weakened the wall of separation metaphor: it did not apply "in every and all respects." In Walz, Burger went further: "No perfect or absolute separation is really possible between church and state." [p.670]

The Court was forced into such a pronouncement by the particularly sticky circumstances of this case:

> The Court has struggled to find a neutral course between the two Religion Clauses, both of which are cast in absolute terms, and either of which, if expanded to a logical extreme, would tend to clash with the other. [p.668]

The line between the two clauses was a "tight rope," Burger said. [p.672] In sum,

either course, taxation of churches or exemption, occasions some degree
of involvement with religion.[p.674]

The Court held that the legislative purpose of the tax exemption statute was
"neither the advancement nor the inhibition of religion." On balance, a tax
exemption that minimally advanced toward establishment was preferable to taxation, which might seriously inhibit free exercise.

A "benevolent neutrality" allowed accommodation but not an impermissible degree of entanglement. If the involvement was excessive or was a continuing one
that called for official surveillance, then the practice constituted establishment. Neither condition existed here.

> Obviously, a direct money subsidy would be a relationship pregnant with
> involvement . . . The grant of a tax exemption is not sponsorship since
> the government does not transfer part of its revenue to churches but sim-
> ply abstains from demanding that the church support the state.[p.675]

*[This statement gave encouragement to sponsors of several plans that would
give state and federal tax exemptions to parents of sectarian school children.
But they misread the Court's use of "degree of involvement." The Court struck
down such a plan in Nyquist(1973): Tax exemption for church property was different from tax exemption for sectarian education. In Nyquist, the Court did
not question the purpose or primary effect; it disallowed tax credits only on
the ground of excessive involvement and found that the practice therefore
amounted to a school subsidy.*

*[The "secular purpose and neutral primary effect" criteria of Schempp
(1963), Epperson (1968), and Allen (1968) continued to be valid, but became
less crucial in Walz. For the first time, the main test was "degree of involvement" of the government in religion, a principle that had been mentioned
in Zorach. This new criterion has continued to be important in establishment
cases, especially in Lemon (1971), Hartington (1972), Meek (1975), and subsequent ones.*

*[The issue of taxes upon churches and their operations is by no means
closed, at either state or local level. Controversies centering on the policies of the Internal Revenue Service have recently emerged. Incidentally, the
Court is currently (summer 1978) considering the issue of whether religious
schools are subject to provisions of the federal labor laws. See TWA, 1977.*

*[The right to grant a tax exemption does not mean that the state may not tax
church property or the income of churches. The right of the state to grant or
withhold exemptions applies also to the income of clergy, but the state may not
tax their religious activities. In Murdock v Pennsylvania, 1943, one of the
many Jehovah's Witnesses cases, the Court ruled (6-3) that government could not
impose a license fee for the right to sell religious literature as an evangelistic activity:*

> *Freedom of speech, freedom of the press, freedom of religion are avail-
> able to all, not merely to those who can pay.[p.111]*

*Appended to this decision was a reversal of an earlier Supreme Court decision
permitting such license fees, which the Murdock ruling contradicted. Compare
with Barnette (1943).]*

Netcong
(and DeKalb, Stein, and Leyden)

In Board of Education v Netcong, 1971, the Court refused to hear an appeal of, and in effect upheld, the New Jersey supreme court's ruling that prayer reading in school during a school-provided period before the formal opening of classes violated the First Amendment, even though the prayers were taken from the Congressional Record and attendance by both pupils and teachers was voluntary.

Three New Jersey courts had held the practice unconstitutional: the trial court, the superior court, and the supreme court—the last in a summary per curiam (unsigned) holding that merely referred to Engel (1962) and Schempp (1963).

[This was the last in a series of such cases to which the Court refused certiorari. Each one attempted a new remedy for, or evasion of, the Schempp decision. In each instance a federal court or a state supreme court had struck the practice down. Some sample cases: DeKalb (Ill.) School District v DeSpain (1967), which banned the "cookie prayer"; and two that banned pupil-initiated prayer—Stein v Olshinsky (N.Y., 1965) and State Commissioner of Education v School Committee (of Leyden, Mass., 1971). (See also Chamberlin, 1964.)

[Attempts to amend the Constitution to permit voluntary attendance at school prayers and Bible reading also collapsed about this time, but have never completely died out. Interest surges from time to time. In the 1930's and 40's the Court had to decide nearly twenty Jehovah's Witnesses cases in ten years before the sect finally won de facto freedom to practice and promulgate its religion. School prayers and devotional Bible reading, the teaching of evolution, and parochiaid seem to be similarly long-lived issues. Remedial, evasive, and/or defiant local practices, legislative enactments, and legal challenges continue on all three fronts. It is not impossible that some accommodation may eventually come, although present odds are against it.]

Lemon/DiCenso

In Lemon v Kurtzman, 1971, (a Pennsylvania case combined with two from Rhode Island, Earley v DiCenso and Robinson v DiCenso) the Court ruled (8-0, in the Pennsylvania case, and 8-1 in the other two) that state laws permitting "purchase of services" from church-related elementary and secondary schools violated the First Amendment Establishment Clause.

The educational services purchased by the state required reimbursement to sectarian schools for textbooks and instructional materials. More strikingly, the state also either paid schools for teacher salaries in specified secular subjects (in Pennsylvania) or directly supplemented teacher salaries for teaching nonreligious subjects (Rhode Island). The Court said it should apply three tests, gleaned respectively from Epperson (1968, teaching evolution), Schempp (1963, morning devotions), and Walz (1970, church tax exemption):

> First, the statute must have a secular legislative purpose; second, its principal or primary effect must be one that neither advances nor inhibits religion; finally, the statute must not foster an excessive entanglement with religion. [p.612]

Thus, all three aspects of a practice were important: its purpose, its effect, and the means by which it achieved that purpose and effect.

Chief Justice Burger, speaking for the Court, did not question the claims in the present cases that the purpose and principal effect of the statutes were to promote general welfare rather than religion. Instead, he pointed to the practical problems involved in determining what was secular teaching in a religious school:

> What would appear to some to be essential to good citizenship might well for others border on or constitute instruction in religion. [p.619]

Such problems led to entanglement. Even in nonideological subjects there were difficulties because of the schools' religious philosophy and atmosphere and because teachers were human and fallible.

As in Walz, it was a question of excessive entanglement, not mere involvement:

> [The] line of separation, far from being a "wall," is a blurred, indistinct, and variable barrier depending on all the circumstances of a particular relationship. [p.614]

Burger cited two examples of excessive entanglement in the Lemon and DiCenso cases, one administrative and the other political. First, the practices in question required

> comprehensive, discriminating, and continuing state surveillance [p.619] . . . [and an] intimate and continuing relationship between church and state. [p.622]

This surveillance and relationship also meant a restriction upon sectarian schools, because they would have to limit their substantial and pervasive religious purpose and activity. The Court had permitted bus transportation, school lunches, public health services, and secular textbooks because they could easily be controlled as to secularity. But teachers, said Burger, "have a substantially different ideological character than books." [p.617]

Second, such laws promoted, at state and local levels,

> political division along religious lines [which] was one of the principal evils against which the First Amendment was intended to protect. [p.622]

The practices would encourage the intrusion of religion into politics in the course of competition between public and sectarian schools each year for a share of the tax dollars allotted to education.

[The Court ignored the contention that denial of aid to parents of sectarian school children inhibited their free exercise of religion. Proponents of the statutes had argued that refusal to permit partial subsidy of teachers put the choice of a religious alternative to public schools beyond the means of many parents. The Court had answered that claim previously in its dicta and would formally confront the issue in Brusca (1972).

[This was the first time that the Court ruled a parochiaid statute unconstitutional. Shortly after Lemon, the Court summarily disallowed a similar Connecticut practice, in Sanders v Johnson (1971). And as a result of Lemon, the attorney general of Massachusetts ruled that a proposed shared-time plan violated the federal Constitution. (See discussion under Meek, 1975.)

[Only a few earlier establishment decisions had not favored sectarian institutions or interests—released time religious education in _McCollum_ (1948) and morning devotions in _Engel_ (1962) and _Schempp_ (1963) being the outstanding examples. In most instances, the Court had tended to encourage proponents of state accommodation to religious institutions: a hospital in _Bradfield_ (1899), sectarian school curricula in _Meyer_ (1923), the existence of sectarian schools in _Pierce_ (1925), busing in _Everson_ (1947), dismissed time religious education in _Zorach_ (1952), textbook loans in _Cochran_ (1930) and _Allen_ (1968), and property tax exemptions in _Walz_ (1970).

[Perhaps as a result of this trend, several states either had or were considering parochiaid laws in addition to those involved in _Lemon_: e.g., vouchers, tuition reimbursements, tax credits, provision of "auxiliary services" (diagnostic and remedial), dual enrollment or shared time (sectarian school pupils attending public school part time), reversed shared time (public school pupils attending religious school part time), and part-time teacher exchanges. All of these were contested, but had not come before the Court.

[Since _Lemon_, some of these issues have reached the Court. In _Wolman_ (1972) the Court summarily affirmed a lower court ruling that struck down a per-pupil grant for parents. In _Hartington_ (1972), the Court permitted leasing of religious school classrooms under ESEA. In _Nyquist_ (1973), it disallowed parent tax credits as well as tuition reimbursements and also struck down public funds for building maintenance and state-mandated services. In _Meek_ (1975), the Court ruled out "auxiliary services" and loan of instructional materials and equipment. In _Walter_ (1977), it sanctioned publicly administered diagnostic services on sectarian school premises and remedial counseling services off the premises, but invalidated other practices.

[In most cases, the state granted funds at the same time that it passed a parochiaid law. Yet when the statute was declared unconstitutional, the states have generally not asked that the money distributed in the intervening two or three years be returned. In fact, some time after _Lemon_ the Court ruled that the schools involved in that case need not repay because the decision had broken new ground.

[This argument was not successful after _Levitt_ (1973), however; the Court felt that neither the state nor the schools in that case had acted in complete ignorance of the possibility of invalidation. Some anti-parochiaid partisans have questioned the intentions of legislators and administrators since _Lemon_ as they have successively replaced invalidated programs with new statutes and appropriations that would not be repaid if found illegal.

[In _Meek_, which dealt with "auxiliary services," the Court expressed second thoughts even about the principal or primary effect of "purchase of services" practices similar to those disallowed in _Lemon_. It said that such programs aided religious enterprises as a primary effect.

[Incidentally, the dissenter in _DiCenso_ was Justice White, who upheld his position, taken in _Allen_, that secular and religious teaching were separable in sectarian schools. The size of the Court's vote in _Lemon_, however, seems to lay to rest one kind of hope raised by his earlier dicta.]

Tilton

In <u>Tilton</u> v <u>Richardson</u>, 1971, the Court upheld (5-4) the constitutionality of Title I of the Federal Higher Education Facilities Act (HEFA) of 1963, which permitted grants for construction of buildings for nonsectarian purposes by church-related (Catholic) colleges (in Connecticut).

The Court did strike down one provision of the act which allowed a college after twenty years to use the building for any purpose, secular or religious. The Court's reasoning was that if the building were then converted to religious use, "the original Federal grant will in part have had the effect of advancing religion."[p.683] Otherwise, as in the <u>Bradfield</u> (1899) hospital precedent, the grants passed the test of secular purpose and neutral primary effect.

Chief Justice Burger announced the Court's decision and the prevailing opinion, since one of the majority wrote a concurring opinion. He said that the entanglement between government and religion in such cases was not excessive. As in <u>Lemon</u> (handed down the same day), Burger referred to the <u>Walz</u> (1970) tax exemption criteria:

> We consider four questions: First does the [HEFA] Act reflect a secular legislative purpose? Second, is the primary effect of the Act to advance or inhibit religion? Third, does the administration of the Act foster an excessive entanglement with religion? Fourth, does the implementation of the Act inhibit free exercise of religion?[p.678]

He listed the distinctions between this case and <u>Lemon</u>, which had dealt with sectarian elementary and secondary schools rather than colleges—

First, the age of the students made an important difference:

> The "affirmative, if not dominant policy" of the instruction in pre-college church schools is to "assure future adherents to a particular faith by having control of their total education at an early age." There is substance to the contention that college students are less impressionable and less susceptible to religious indoctrination.[p.685]

Second, there was little danger of deep or long-term administrative entanglement:

> The necessity for intensive government surveillance is diminished . . . by the nonideological character of the aid . . . [whereas] teachers are not necessarily religiously neutral . . . [Furthermore, this is] a one-time single purpose construction grant . . . Inspection as to use is a minimal contact.[pp.687,688]

In addition, college students are not normally drawn from only one major local district, so that divisive, religiously partisan battles are less likely to be encouraged by aid to sectarian colleges than to sectarian schools. Thus the degree of political involvement was no more excessive in the case of college buildings than was administrative entanglement.

Third, evidence showed that the purpose and atmosphere of the four colleges in question were not entirely permeated by religion; like many other private and public colleges, they

> are characterized by a high degree of academic freedom and seek to evoke

free and critical responses from their students. . . . [Their] predom-
inant higher education mission is to provide their students with a secular education. [pp.686,687]

*[This is not true of all church-related colleges, of course. In Horace Mann
League (1969) the Court had refused certiorari in a similar Maryland case. The
state supreme court had previously ruled that three of four applicant sectarian
colleges were too pervasively religious to qualify for state construction
grants. Criteria produced at that trial have become influential. Some of the
colleges' disabilities: religious requirements for student entrance and faculty appointment; compulsory sectarian theology courses; and standards of religious belief and practice for their students, faculty, and policy-making
boards.]*

Burger noted the criteria within which sectarian colleges might be eligible
for government aid: 1) no religious test for faculty or students, 2) no required attendance at religious services, 3) no required religion courses that
tend to indoctrinate, and 4) commitment to academic freedom and professional
standards.

*[These criteria are consistent with the dicta of Schempp (1963), which ap-
proved the study of religion "when presented objectively as part of a secular
program of education." Most state colleges have applied the Tilton criteria to
their own religion courses. They feel that such courses should be secular in
purpose and not seek to indoctrinate or proselytize and that the faculty should
include people from more than one religious community. The Court has consistently held that although sectarian schools are of necessity pervasively religious, church-related colleges need not be.*

*[Incidentally, Justice White, who wrote the concurring opinion, did not see
the difference between such aid to schools (Lemon) and to colleges (Tilton):
Both should receive aid for secular purposes. He dissented in Lemon, but was
with the prevailing side here. Conversely, the dissenters in Tilton also saw
no difference between sectarian schools and colleges sponsored by sectarian interests, but said that neither one should receive aid.*

*[Two issues were involved: First, does a sectarian school have separable
secular activities or does it not? White said it does. Second, should the
Court ignore religious issues in such cases and decide them only on the basis
of equal treatment (the Fourteenth Amendment) under general welfare, or should
the Court balance general welfare interests against those of religious freedom
(under the First Amendment)? The Court favored the latter approach.*

*[Those interested the issue of governmental support of sectarian colleges
point out that the HEFA of 1963, which was challenged in Tilton, incorporated
some of the provisions of the earlier National Defense Education Act (NDEA) of
1958. This earlier act intended to improve educational resources to compete
with Russia, which had launched the first space projectile—the Sputnik. Not
only did NDEA of 1958 include funds for students and programs in science and
the humanities at sectarian colleges, but it also gave grants for religious
study at seminaries. Church-related colleges have benefited from still other
programs designed for the general welfare: e.g., urban renewal, surplus property donations, and programs of the Office of Economic Opportunity (OEO).*

[The taxpayer's right to challenge a program such as HEFA results from Flast (1968). The specific issue in Tilton was federal grants for church-related college buildings. In Hunt (1973), the issue was state aid for such a purpose, though not through a grant. Roemer (1976) broadened the area of permissible government grants to sectarian colleges—far beyond building construction and participation in specific governmental programs such as NDEA and OEO.

[A related issue is before the lower courts in Pennsylvania and may eventually reach the Supreme Court. The suit challenges the transfer of the properties of an army hospital to a Bible college. And a suit in Minnesota objects to the leasing of state university premises to the YWCA, a religious organization.]

Brusca
(and Barrera, Luetkemeyer, and Paster)

In Brusca v State Board of Education, 1972, the Court affirmed without comment a three-judge U. S. district court ruling that a state constitution's prohibition against the use of public funds for any indirect aid to sectarian schools violated neither the Free Exercise Clause of the federal Constitution's First Amendment nor the Equal Protection Clause of its Fourteenth.

At issue were several of Missouri's strong and specific constitutional provisions: e.g.,

> Neither the general assembly, nor any county, city, town, township, school district or other municipal corporation, shall ever make an appropriation or pay from any public fund whatever, anything in aid of any religious creed, church or sectarian purpose, or to help to support or sustain any private or public school or academy, seminary, college, university, or other institution of learning controlled by any religious creed, church, or sectarian denomination whatever. [Art.IX, sect.8]

The federal district court dismissed the suit against the state. In doing so, District Judge Regan issued a memorandum opinion, saying that parents did not have a right to public funds with which to take advantage of the free choice of education guaranteed them in Pierce (1925). The federal Constitution permitted, but did not mandate, government funding of certain nonideological services for sectarian school pupils.

It is true, Regan said, that the state may not act to interfere with free exercise and that the state may refrain from acting in order to maintain a position of neutrality where free exercise might tend toward establishment. But the state may not act to subsidize free exercise—which would certainly constitute establishment of religion.

[The Court's subsequent opinions echoed Regan's words. (See Nyquist, 1973.) And in October, 1977, the Court refused to hear an appeal from a federal court ruling that the Pennsylvania state constitution's ban on tax aid for parochial schools did not violate their free exercise or equal protection rights.

[Nevertheless, sectarian interests continued to challenge Missouri's constitution as interpreted by the courts. The state constitution, partisans held, was illegally preventing schools from receiving a variety of benefits that the U.S. Supreme Court had approved under the federal Constitution. Some specific

issues that they raised over the years reached the Supreme Court, in the following cases:

[In Wheeler v Barrera, 1974, the Court ruled (8-1) that local public school districts were not required to provide ESEA 1965 funds for remedial services at sectarian schools nor to send public school teachers there (see discussion under Flast, 1968). Catholic school officials in Missouri had demanded that ESEA programs be held on their premises, but public school authorities said that would violate the state constitution. Their offer of "comparable" off-the-premises services was refused. (This premises dispute arose in other First Amendment cases: e.g., released time religious education in McCollum, 1968, and auxiliary services in Walter, 1977.)

[In upholding the lower court's ruling, the Court, speaking through Justice Blackmun, said that ESEA of 1965 was to be administered equally, but not so as to violate state laws, since ESEA funds became state funds. (In some instances, Congress has enacted "by-pass" amendments that allow a federal agency to provide certain services directly to sectarian schools in states whose constitutions prohibit the schools from receiving such aid from the state.)

[The Court did not rule in Barrera on the issue originally raised by Flast, who wanted to challenge the federal constitutionality of ESEA of 1965. It refused to consider whether sending public school teachers and pupils to sectarian school premises violated the Establishment Clause. (See discussion under Walter.)

[In Luetkemeyer v Kaufman, 1974, the Court summarily affirmed (7-2) a federal district court's decision that Missouri could refuse to provide bus transportation for sectarian school pupils if that practice violated the state's constitution. The

> *long established policy of the State of Missouri, which insists upon a degree of separation of church and state to probably a higher degree than that required by the First Amendment[364 FSupp 386]*

was a more compelling state interest than public welfare benefits to the children. (See Everson, 1947.)

[In Reynolds v Paster, 1975, the Court denied certiorari to an appeal from the Missouri supreme court's decision that the loan of textbooks to sectarian school pupils also violated the state's constitution. (See Allen, 1968.)

[All these Missouri cases dealt with parochiaid for schools, not colleges. As a result of the Roemer (1976) decision, which sanctioned grants to sectarian colleges for general, unspecified secular purposes, the Missouri supreme court interpreted the state constitution to permit tuition reimbursements to students at church-related colleges, but laid down conditions even more stringent than those required in Tilton (1971) and in Roemer.]

Yoder

In Wisconsin v Yoder, 1972, the Court upheld (7-0; one of the seven dissented in part only) a Wisconsin supreme court ruling that children of the Old Order Amish and Conservative Amish Mennonite sects might leave school after the eighth grade regardless of age, giving to members of the two sects an exclusive exemption from a state law requiring school attendance until age sixteen.

These sects regarded the public high school's social milieu, teachings, and values (which emphasized worldliness, competitiveness, and scientific and intellectual knowledge) as "endangering their own salvation and that of their children"[p.209] as well as the existence of the sect. They were concerned not to be "conformed to this world" (Rom.12:2) or "unequally yoked with unbelievers" (2 Cor.6:14).

Chief Justice Burger, speaking for the Court, said that the state's interest in and right to impose compulsory education was "by no means absolute."[p.215] The interest was not sufficiently "compelling" *[the test announced in Sherbert (1963)]*. In this instance such an imposition violated the Free Exercise Clause, as well as the "traditional interest of parents with respect to the religious upbringing of their children"[p.214] *[the principle of Pierce (1925)]*.

The state's argument had five discernable aspects. First, the state said that children and society would suffer if the children did not attend school beyond the eighth grade. Burger dismissed this contention on the ground that the sects had produced responsible citizens for many generations:

> The record strongly indicates that accommodating the religious objections of the Amish by forgoing one, or at most two, additional years of compulsory education will not impair the physical or mental health of the child, or result in an inability to be self-supporting or to discharge the duties and responsibilities of citizenship, or in any other way to detract from the welfare of society.[p.234]

[This did not contradict the Court's position on compulsory elementary education. In Donner (1951) the Court had sanctioned a statute requiring attendance at an approved elementary school even if that interfered with religious beliefs. Secondary school education was not at issue.]

In a second, and related, argument, the state maintained that Reynolds (1878) had placed religious actions (as opposed to beliefs) outside the protection of the Free Exercise Clause. Burger replied that

> only those interests of the highest order not otherwise served can overbalance legitimate claims to the free exercise of religion.[p.214]

[The criteria for limiting religious practice were two: a compelling governmental interest (e.g., public safety) and the absence of an alternative that did not restrict religious practice. See also Anderson, 1972.]

Third, the state asserted that the compulsory attendance regulation was religiously neutral since it applied equally to everyone. The Court said that the rule applied with unequal force to these people because it "unduly burdens [their] free exercise of religion."[p.221]

A fourth claim was that such an exemption might violate the Establishment Clause. Burger recalled the dicta in Walz (1970), which listed the main threats to establishment as "sponsorship, financial support, and active involvement of the sovereign in religious activity."[p.234, footnote 22] None of these conditions existed in Yoder sufficient to deny free exercise.

A fifth state contention was that this was not a religious but a philosophical or cultural issue. Burger said that, quite to the contrary, what was at stake was the free exercise of religion—religion in the traditional, denominational sense. "Three centuries as an identifiable religious sect," he said, separated this case from individuals or groups who might seek exemption from compulsory education because of their commitment to some

> recently discovered . . . "progressive" or more enlightened process for rearing children for modern life.[p.235]

More specifically, the Court stated that

> If the Amish asserted their claims because of their subjective evaluation and rejection of the contemporary secular values accepted by the majority, much as Thoreau [did] . . . at Walden Pond, their claims would not rest on a religious basis. . . . [T]he traditional way of life of the Amish is not merely a matter of personal preference, but one of deep religious conviction, shared by an organized group . . . [I]t is in response to their literal interpretation of the Biblical injunction from the Epistle of Paul to the Romans, "Be not conformed to this world." [p.216]

[As Justice Douglas pointed out in his concurring opinion, which dissented only in part, the Court seemed to return to a conservative definition of religion in this case. It appeared to contradict the broad definition it used to grant exemptions from compulsory military service to conscientious objectors, in Seeger (1965) and Welsh (1970).

[In those two cases, membership in a sect was not necessary for a religious exemption from the law. An individual might base his/her objection on beliefs that were purely personal—and only philosophical or sociological in source and content. In Yoder, such a person was explicitly excluded from religious exemption. (See discussion under Welsh, especially concerning moral education.)

[The concessions to sectarians in Yoder may have implications for the school calendar: e.g., should schools schedule make-up, enrichment, or examination activities on Saturday without special arrangements for Christian sabbatarians and Orthodox Jews? As for religion, must schools insist on critical thinking?]

Wolman

In Essex v Wolman, 1972, the Court, without a hearing or opinion, summarily affirmed (8-1) a federal district court ruling that an Ohio law providing payment of $90 to parents of nonpublic school pupils to offset expenses for tuition, books, lab fees, bus fares, etc., violated the Establishment Clause.

The district court had held that the effect of the grant was to serve a limited, predominantly religious group—approximately twelve per cent of the Ohio student population—of which ninety-five per cent attended Catholic schools. The case was not similar to Everson (1947, busing) or to Allen (1968, textbooks), said the Court, for they had merely extended to sectarian school pupils what was already available to public school pupils. It was closer to Lemon (1971, purchase of services), because the "substantial beneficiary can only be organized religion."[342 FSupp 413]

The district court had also rejected the contention that the manner of payment—to parents rather than to schools—would not lead to excessive entanglement. The court answered that payment to the parent for transmittal to the denominational school does not have a cleansing effect and somehow cause the funds to lose their identity as public funds. While the ingenuity of man is apparently limitless, the Court has held with unvarying regularity that one may not do by indirection what is forbidden directly.[342 FSupp 415]

[Although the Court did not hear arguments in this case, it did so in a similar instance, Nyquist (1973).]

Hartington

In Nebraska Board of Education v Hartington School District, 1972, the Court (7-2) refused to review and thereby let stand a state supreme court ruling that it was not unconstitutional for a public school district to lease classrooms in a religious school building, with funds from ESEA of 1965, for remedial classes that included educationally deprived children from both public and sectarian schools. *[See Flast (1968).]*

The state court saw no "excessive entanglement," since the leased property was "under the control of public school authorities and the instruction is secular and nonsectarian."[195 NW2d 163] The Supreme Court refused to decide the constitutionality of ESEA itself, which was challenged because it included benefits for sectarian school children. *[See also Barrera (1974).]*

Anderson

In Laird v Anderson, 1972, the Court refused to hear an appeal from, and in effect upheld, a lower court decision that mandatory chapel attendance at national military academies violated the Establishment Clause.

The two-man majority of the federal appeals court was not convinced of a military necessity for attendance that was so compelling as to warrant in-infringement upon religious liberty *[see also Yoder, 1972]*. Nor were they convinced by the claim that the purpose was secular—to develop "that sensitivity to religious emotion required of a military leader."[466F2d 299]

They agreed that even if the military purpose had been truly secular, mandatory attendance was not called for. The two judges reasoned differently toward this conclusion. Justice Leventhal said that the practice violated the Establishment Clause, and he quoted with approval from Justice Brennan's concurring opinion in Schempp (1963):

> Government may not employ religious means to serve secular interests, however legitimate they may be, at least without the clearest demonstration that nonreligious means will not suffice.[466 F2d 302]

Chief Justice Bazelon acknowledged that the U.S. Supreme Court had moved away from the "strict neutrality" cited in Everson (1947), which prohibited aid to "one religion or all religions." It had substituted the "accommodation" and "benign neutrality" of Walz (1970). Such accommodation was not by religion to the state, however, but rather by the state to religion, he said. And even then, the state was to make concessions to religion only where insistence on "no establishment" would seriously harm free exercise: e.g., where a property tax might force a church out of existence, or where servicemen could not worship if the military did not provide chaplains. Bazelon said the military practice at the academies violated the Free Exercise Clause as well as the Establishment Clause, because it demanded accommodation of religion to the state.

[One must keep in mind that this discussion of the judges' opinions comes from their dicta. If there is a question as to how the Supreme Court feels about the actual ruling of a lower court when it denies certiorari, there is even less justification for attributing the Court's approval to a lower court's dicta—unless a Supreme Court opinion cites the dicta in a later case, as was true with the words of both Leventhal and Bazelon.]

Norwood

In Norwood v Harrison, 1973, the Court unanimously declared unconstitutional a Mississippi program that provided free textbooks for pupils of private non-sectarian schools and academies because virtually all of them had racially discriminatory policies.

[This was not a religious issue, but the case has possible implications for parochiaid legislation. Most programs aimed primarily at aid for (pupils of) sectarian schools are framed to benefit all nonpublic nonprofit schools, religious and nonreligious. This inclusiveness emphasizes the secular functions of sectarian schools. They may thus be helped or hampered by the character of the nonsectarian schools with which they associate themselves in these programs. The Norwood ruling drives a wedge between permissible aid to nondiscriminatory sectarian schools and impermissible aid to discriminatory schools of whatever stripe.

[As for racially discriminatory sectarian schools, in February, 1978, the Court refused to review a federal appeals court ruling that the Free Exercise Clause did not protect a Florida sectarian school's policy of refusing to enroll black children. (See also Runyon, 1976).

[In general, proponents of parochiaid continue to press for expansion of aid to sectarian schools, their pupils, or parents through many and varied avenues. Conversely, opponents continue to challenge existing parochiaid practices; some plaintiffs have recently argued that textbook loans foster and perpetuate racial segregation.

[In Norwood, benefits of the disallowed act had gone directly to pupils and only indirectly to the schools. In Bob Jones (1974) and Runyon, the Court extended the Norwood ban directly to the racially discriminatory colleges and schools by withdrawing their tax exempt status.

[The language used in the Norwood opinion was "racial or other invidious discrimination." [p.467] Some opponents of bus transportation and textbook loans to sectarian schools have since suggested that religious imbalance in sectarian schools might constitute de facto invidious discrimination. The Court has not faced such a challenge, however.]

Nyquist/Sloan/Levitt

(also <u>Grit</u>, <u>Franchise Tax Board</u>, <u>Marburger</u>, and <u>Minn</u>. CLU)

On the same day as <u>Norwood</u> (above) and <u>Hunt</u> (below), the Court struck down several school parochiaid practices, in three related decisions: a) <u>Committee for Public Education and Religious Liberty</u> (PEARL) v <u>Nyquist</u> (combining four New York cases), b) <u>Sloan</u> v <u>Lemon</u> (two Pennsylvania cases), and c) <u>Levitt</u> v <u>PEARL</u> (three New York cases).

The Court invalidated four kinds of practices: first, a New York law that provided direct grants to nonpublic schools (nearly all of them sectarian and Catholic) for maintenance and repair of facilities serving the health, welfare, and safety of pupils (<u>Nyquist</u>, 9-0).

Second, it ruled out tuition reimbursements that the state gave to parents of sectarian—but not secular—school students in both New York and Pennsylvania (<u>Nyquist</u> and <u>Sloan</u>, 6-3).

Third, it declared unconstitutional the practice of offering tax relief as an alternative to tuition reimbursement for such parents, in New York (<u>Nyquist</u>, 6-3).

Fourth, the Court also struck down direct reimbursements to New York nonpublic schools for state-mandated testing, record keeping, and reporting (<u>Levitt</u>, 8-1).

Chief Justice Burger spoke for the Court in <u>Levitt</u>; Justice Powell, in <u>Nyquist</u> and <u>Sloan</u>. Of the three cases, <u>Nyquist</u> got the fullest treatment because its provisions were the most inclusive. Again, the stumbling block was the Establishment Clause. And again, the three criteria came from <u>Lemon</u> (1971): a secular purpose of the laws, their neutral primary effect, and minimal church-state entanglement. The issue of free exercise was not important.

[The Court had by now settled upon guidelines for applying its criteria in parochiaid cases: On the one hand, to give financial relief to church-related schools or to its pupils' parents would have a purpose and primary effect that tended toward establishment of religion. On the other hand, to deny the benefits of general welfare legislation to children whose religious beliefs sent them to sectarian schools tended to interfere with the right to free exercise of religion—and the right to equal protection.

[The Court had to make a series of decisions. First, which practices supported the school or parents and which were for the benefit of the child? Second, if a practice benefited both the child's welfare and the finances of the school and/or parent, which one was the "primary" effect? The Court had also used the expression "direct and immediate" effect and permitted some indirect and remote benefits to sectarian schools: "An indirect and incidental effect beneficial to religious institutions has never been thought a sufficient defect to warrant the invalidation of a state law."[p.775]

[Third, even if the purpose and primary effect of the practice neither advanced nor inhibited religion, did government have to become "excessively" involved in policing the practice to make sure that there were no violations? Excessive entanglement might be administrative—too detailed and/or continual surveillance—or politically divisive along religious lines.

[Fourth, in order to determine whether a practice needed such surveillance, the Court had to take into consideration the nature of the service provided for the pupils, where they took place (on the premises or not), and who provided them (public or sectarian school employees). (These last two questions become important in Meek, 1975, and Walter, 1977.)]

In Nyquist, the New York law provided maintenance grants to the schools and a choice of either tuition reimbursements or tax credits to parents. The Court conceded the law's purposes to be secular and valuable: to provide a healthy and safe educational environment, to encourage pluralism and diversity of educational alternatives, and to lessen the financial burden on the state by retaining pupils in nonpublic schools.

The law failed the second test, however. The Court held its primary effect to be the advancement of religion. Justice Powell specifically rejected the argument that maintaining facilities and either reimbursing or granting tax relief to parents were like busing pupils (as in Everson, 1947) or like providing secular textbooks (as in Allen, 1968). In those cases the state provided the welfare service generally, to all pupils rather than to only those in nonpublic schools, as here. In Everson and Allen, help for sectarian schools was indirect and incidental, while in Nyquist it was primary. The effect, said Powell, "is to subsidize and advance the religious mission of sectarian schools." [p.779]

More important, he said, in Everson and Allen the state could easily restrict the aid to secular functions related to the schools. In Nyquist, there was no way to insure that funds would not be used to maintain religious facilities rather than that portion of space and time allotted to secular activities. Nor was there any way to prevent parents from passing on their reimbursement grants or tax benefits to the sectarian schools. Administration of the law did not permit surveillance; the question of whether involvement was excessive was academic.

These arguments applied to tax benefits as well as to grants, said Powell. It made no difference in the Court's eyes whether the benefits were called "credits," "modifications," "deductions," or "forgiveness." Like the reimbursements to the school or the parents, the "money involved represents a charge made upon the state for the purpose of religious education." [p.791]

Furthermore, the Court clearly differentiated between income tax benefits and the property tax exemptions for church property upheld in Walz (1970), on several grounds. Property tax exemptions had a long accepted and harmless history. They balanced the power to inhibit religion by taxation; they tended to lessen entanglement between church and state; and they applied to all charitable and educational institutions as well as to churches. On all these counts, income tax benefits were different or even completely opposite: the income tax exemption was new, would increase government involvement in religion, and would benefit religious institutions almost exclusively.

Thus, although the law in Nyquist passed the first test, secular purpose, it failed on the ground of primary or principal effect. As for the third criterion, in addition to the administrative morass, the law carried "grave potential for entanglement in the broader sense of continuing political strife over aid to religion."[p.794] Increasing appropriations would probably be requested each year, Powell said.

> Moreover, the State itself, concededly anxious to avoid assuming the burden of educating children now in private and parochial schools, has strong motivation for increasing this aid as public school costs rise and population increases.[p.797]

Thus, he felt, political factionalism along religious lines would increase.

In Sloan, the Court declared the Pennsylvania "Parent Reimbursement Act for Nonpublic Education" unconstitutional because "we find no constitutionally significant distinctions between this law and the one declared invalid today in Nyquist."[p.828]

In Levitt, proponents said the state was buying "auxiliary services." But as in Nyquist and Sloan (and unlike Everson and Allen), there was no guarantee that the aid for testing, record keeping, and reporting would be applied only to secular functions of sectarian schools. The largest item was the internal, teacher-prepared and teacher-administered, tests in all courses. They were "state-mandated" in the sense that the state required an internal testing program for evaluating pupils' achievement and also required periodic reports.

The Court said that the case was similar to Lemon. The law provided, in effect, for paying part of the teachers' salaries, because testing was "an integral part of the teaching process." And the fact that the state set educational (or, for that matter, building maintenance) standards did not require it to pay for meeting those standards, the Court felt.

Furthermore, internal tests would need continuing state inspection to ensure that they were not sectarian—even in mathematics, science, and foreign language test questions. Thus, excessive entanglement, even more than purpose or primary effect, was the barrier in Levitt. [This problem was resolved in Walter, 1977, by separating internal and external testing.]

[In a separate case (Grit v Wolman) on the same day, the Court summarily affirmed a lower court decision that prohibited tax credits for parents of religious school children in Ohio. Nevertheless, various states continued to defend similar practices through the courts for the next few years. Since then, the battle for this kind of parochiaid has shifted to the Congressional arena.

[In Franchise Tax Board v United Americans for Public Schools, 1974, the Court (6-3) affirmed without comment a federal district court ruling that a California plan which gave income tax credits to parents of nonpublic school children was unconstitutional.

[In Marburger v Public Funds, 1974, the Court (6-3) also summarily affirmed a decision by a federal district court that struck down a similar New Jersey law. Like Nyquist and Levitt, it provided for reimbursement to sectarian schools for supplies and "auxiliary services." It also offered payment to parents for money spent on "secular textbooks, instructional materials, and supplies." The dissenting justices felt that the arguments should be heard because of the new issues—which the Court later did examine in Meek (1975).

[In _Minnesota_ v _Minnesota CLU_, 1975, the Court, without dissent, refused to review a judgment that declared unconstitutional a statute which provided state income tax credits and tuition reimbursements for parents of nonpublic school pupils. (In 1976 the Minnesota legislature passed a slightly different act, which is before the lower courts.)

[After the federal district court had ruled in _Levitt_ that the state law was unconstitutional, and before the Supreme Court acted on the appeal, New York passed a new law allowing sectarian schools to receive the funds in the interim. This new law was also challenged; but not until December, 1977, did the Court hold (6-3) that it too was unconstitutional. The Court had previously refused certiorari in a second _Sloan_ case, where the lower courts had denied payment of aid to sectarian schools while the first case was pending. (See discussion under _Lemon_).

[Incidentally, one of the Court's criteria for excessive entanglement is, as we have seen, the potential for political divisiveness along religious lines. The Court's invalidation of various kinds of parochiaid has itself contributed to such divisiveness, largely because some cynical politicians have on occasion seen fit to exploit the issue and inflame its partisans against the Court.

[The PEARL group in _Nyquist_ and _Levitt_ included, among many others, the three most frequent separationist litigators: the American Civil Liberties Union (ACLU); the American Jewish Congress (AJC); and Americans United for Separation of Church and State (AU), formerly Protestants and Other Americans United (POAU). (Some constituents of PEARL represent religious sects; a current controversy arises from attempts to subject such religious groups to lobbying regulations.)]

Hunt (and _Clayton_)

In _Hunt_ v _McNair_, 1973, (handed down the same day as _Norwood_ and _Nyquist_, above) the Court upheld (6-3) a South Carolina law that authorized state bond issues (but not the state's credit—it would merely make income on the bonds tax free) to help private colleges and universities build nonreligious facilities, although some of the institutions were controlled by religious sects.

The criteria derived from _Lemon_ (1971). The purpose was secular, and the primary or principal effect neither advanced nor inhibited religion. The law did not foster excessive state entanglement with religion either administratively or politically.

The Court was satisfied that in the church-related colleges the education program was not sectarian, there were no religious qualifications for accepting students or hiring faculty, and the religion of the majority of the students reflected that of the surrounding area. Speaking through Justice Powell, the Court said that the case was similar to _Bradfield_ (1899), the hospital case, and to _Tilton_ (1971), which established the criteria for construction grants to sectarian colleges. _[See also _Roemer_ (1976).]_

[The _Hunt_ decision was a formal declaration of a position of the Court at which it had hinted earlier: _Clayton_ v _Kervick_, 1971, appealed the New Jersey state treasurer's refusal to release state funds for bonding new buildings at private colleges. A state court ruled for the treasurer. The U.S. Supreme

Court, implying that bonding was like the Tilton grant, sent the case back for a new decision.]

Bob Jones (and Runyon)

In Bob Jones University v Simon, 1974, the Court ruled (7-1) that the Internal Revenue Service could legally end an institution's tax exempt status for otherwise deductible charitable contributions because of the institution's discrimination on the basis of race.

[The decision extends to colleges and to tax exemptions the position taken in Norwood (1973), which forbade state aid to private academies on the same ground. Possible implications for religion came from the language of that decision: "racial or other invidious discrimination."

[In Runyon v McCrary, 1976, the Court ruled (7-2) that exclusion of Negroes/ black people from private, commercial, nonsectarian academies (in Mississippi) violated the Civil Rights Act of 1866. A postwar enactment, it was interested only in the rights of black people and did not address discrimination on the basis of sex or religion.

[Shortly after the Runyon decision, the Mississippi Citizen's Council donated seven such schools (in Jackson) to the Southern Baptist Church. Thereupon, the Internal Revenue Service was petitioned to cancel the church's tax exempt status. The case is still (summer, 1978) pending, but see discussion under Norwood.

[An interesting related issue results from the clash of religious scruples and women's rights in education. The government has threatened colleges with loss of federal funds if they discriminate against women. Brigham Young University (Mormon) refused to hire or to accept as students women who were "immorally pregnant," had abortions, or were in sexually unsegregated off-campus housing. In June, 1978, the government waived the housing stipulation.]

Meek (and Wolman 2)

In Meek v Pittenger, 1975, the Court struck down (6-3) a Pennsylvania law that provided state aid to nonpublic schools in the form of a) the loan of instructional materials (periodicals, maps, recordings, films) and A-V and laboratory equipment and b) the provision of "auxiliary services" (counseling, testing, and remedial classes). At the same time, the Court (in a different alignment) upheld the part of the law that loaned secular textbooks to nonpublic school pupils, as in Allen (1968).

The Court, through Justice Stewart, applied the threefold test of Lemon (1971): secular purpose, neutral primary effect, and minimal involvement. Textbooks passed those tests, but other loans did not satisfy the second criterion. Whereas pupils used textbooks at home, other materials and equipment remained on the school premises:

> The direct loan of instructional materials and equipment has the unconstitutional primary effect of advancing religion because of the predominantly religious character of the schools (75%) benefiting from the Act. [p.363]

In contrast, Stewart said, textbook loans, bus transportation, school lunch-es, and public health facilities were

> secular and non-ideological services unrelated to the primary, religious oriented educational function of the secondary school [p.364]

and benefits to the schools were indirect and incidental.

Loan of materials and equipment failed the third test as well. Religion permeated the schools, and the state would need continual surveillance to see that the equipment and materials were not used for sectarian purposes.

Similarly, the "auxiliary services" failed both the primary effect and ex-cessive entanglement criteria. Even though outside personnel would be adminis-tering these services, they would be doing so within the school's pervasively religious atmosphere. As with loans, this practice required constant, entang-ling surveillance, to see that counseling and remedial instruction did not be-come ideological; for teachers were susceptible to bias, as the Court had sug-gested in Lemon. The religious school might become the primary beneficiary.

The Court here officially disposed of the argument that secular activities of sectarian schools were separable. Stewart quoted with approval from Justice Brennan's concurring opinion in Lemon:

> The secular education those schools provide goes hand in hand with the religious mission that is the only reason for the school's existence. Within the institution, the two are inextricably intertwined. [p.366]

Furthermore, the Court said that, as in Lemon and Nyquist (1973), such grants promoted political strife along religious lines because of competition for the state's funds. Political entanglement compounded administrative entan-glement.

[These invalidating decisions in Meek made more explicit and broadened the proscriptions of Nyquist and Sloan (1973). Conversely, it narrowed the poten-tial area for permissible aid to sectarian schools. A bit of light for accom-modationists, however, shone through a chink in the Court's dicta about auxil-iary services. (See Walter, 1977, which picked up a hint about separating the diagnostic from the remedial services.)

[This was the third Pennsylvania law struck down in four years. The state enacted each new law as the Supreme Court invalidated the previous one, in an attempt to adapt to the new restrictions and to keep money flowing to the non-public (sectarian) schools. Lemon eliminated "purchase of services"—reim-bursement to schools for instructional materials and teacher salaries. Sloan (and Nyquist) ruled out tuition reimbursements and tax credits to parents. Meek invalidated grants to schools for auxiliary services and for loan of ma-terials and equipment. The legislature thereupon enacted a new law—to con-form to (say friends) or circumvent (say enemies) the Meek ruling. This law was affected by the Walter decision.

[Ohio followed the same process as Pennsylvania, as did many other states. In Wolman v Essex (referred to as Wolman 2), 1975, the Court unanimously per curiam struck down a federal district court's approval of an Ohio plan for state support of nonpublic school auxiliary services. It was remanded for further consideration in view of the Court's decision a week earlier in Meek.

The federal district court then decided that the case was not distinguishable from Meek and ruled the Ohio law unconstitutional, whereupon Ohio enacted a new statute. This time the Court took Ohio's law first, and the result was Walter. The process continues. Those parts of the Walter decision that invalidated certain parochiaid practices brought forth yet another legislative enactment.

[The Meek case has implications for some aspects of ESEA of 1965 (see Flast, 1968). The special instructional materials and equipment and auxiliary services provided within sectarian schools that were disallowed in Meek were intended for educationally handicapped pupils, according to the statute. These pupils were the same ones who benefited from ESEA, most of whose funds go into auxiliary services and equipment loans of the type struck down here. The decision encouraged opponents of ESEA, who filed a suit in federal district court challenging ESEA programs conducted on sectarian school premises.

[In addition, it has been argued that Meek implies at least partial approval of shared time (dual enrollment), a practice fostered by ESEA administrators, because the Meek dicta sanctioned the provision of auxiliary services in public schools to pupils of sectarian schools. A further inference from Meek's ruling is that it disapproves of reversed shared time because it said that auxiliary services, even when performed by public school personnel, were not clearly non-ideological if administered on the premises of a sectarian school.]

Roemer

In Roemer v Maryland Board of Public Works, 1976, the Court ruled (5-4) that Maryland could give "noncategorical" institutional grants to church-affiliated liberal arts colleges for general secular purposes that were not covered (in any category) by specific legislation.

The state plan called for annual payments and reports, and it applied to all nonpublic colleges and universities, sectarian and nonsectarian. To qualify, church-related institutions had to offer more than only theological degree programs, and they could not use the money for sectarian purposes. Challenged in Roemer were four Catholic colleges. A Methodist college that was originally part of the suit eliminated itself by becoming completely secular.

Justice Blackmun, speaking for the prevailing plurality, found that the program passed the threefold test of Lemon (1971): secular purpose, neutral primary effect, and minimal involvement.

The main issue was whether the four colleges were so pervasively religious that their sectarian functions could not be separated out for funding. Here Blackmun applied the Tilton (1971) criteria: the absence of religious tests for faculty recruitment and student admissions; the absence of required attendance at religious services and at indoctrinating religion courses; and a commitment to academic freedom, even in the religion courses. To be characterized as pervasively religious, a college would have to violate several of these criteria: it was the general character of the institution that would govern the decision.

The majority of the Court found that although the colleges in question did have varying religious aspects, those features did not add up to pervasiveness.

For instance, the colleges were, on balance, relatively free of religious tests. Religion was not a factor in student admissions, although it might be in awarding scholarships. Religion was only one consideration in recruiting the faculty, which included non-Catholics.

As for evangelism, the Court felt that there was no general atmosphere of indoctrination. Faculty might choose to start classes with a prayer and to wear clerical garb, but these practices were not mandatory nor consistent. Religious services were voluntary. And the prevailing commitment was felt to be to academic freedom. Although there were mandatory religion courses, they were merely supplementary to the academic degree program. The four colleges were not uniform in their practices, but they fell within this characterization.

Since the colleges were not pervasively religious, said the Court, it was possible to separate out secular purposes and primary effects for the use of public grant money. Such a separation also reduced the need for involvement of the state in college affairs. And political divisiveness was not a threat because funds went to all the nonpublic colleges in the state, based only on enrollment figures.

The Roemer decisions broadened considerably the ruling of Tilton, which had sanctioned grants only for the construction of secular buildings at sectarian colleges. As in Tilton, the vote was close and the majority was split. The official opinion carried only three signatures; two other justices filed a concurring opinion. The four dissenters filed three opinions.

The concurring opinion rejected the use of "degree of involvement" as a test on two grounds. It was circular (it took surveillance to ensure that no surveillance was needed), and it was redundant (the criterion—religious pervasiveness—was the same for both primary effect and entanglement).

The various dissents objected to the degree of religious permeation and to the lack of control over the compulsory religion courses. The justices felt that the secular functions of the colleges were not sufficiently separated. In addition, Justice Stevens stressed his concern over the

> pernicious tendency of a state subsidy to tempt religious schools to compromise their religious mission without wholly abandoning it. [p.775]

[Because of the Court's fragmented vote and its narrow reliance on the specific character of the individual Maryland colleges, the transferability of the ruling as precedent was somewhat limited. Nevertheless, Roemer did expand the area for state aid to sectarian colleges. It has stimulated some states to provide grants to church-related colleges and to their students.

[In October, 1977, the Court summarily affirmed lower court rulings that upheld state tuition grants to students in sectarian colleges in Tennessee and in North Carolina. The Court denied certiorari to an appeal from the Missouri supreme court's decision which approved tuition grants to students at church-affiliated colleges, provided that the boards of directors were independent of the church. In so ruling, the Missouri court cited Roemer and reinterpreted the state's ultra-separationist constitution (see Brusca, 1972). In Louisiana, where a suit had been pending, the parties agreed that on the basis of Roemer the state might release per-student grant funds to nonpublic colleges, six of them church-related. Pressure for college tuition tax credits is growing, at

both federal and state levels.

[The Court's expansion of permissible aid to sectarian colleges accompanied an increasing restriction of the area for government aid to sectarian elementary and secondary schools (and to their pupils and parents): Tilton, the same day as Lemon; Hunt, the same day as Nyquist; and Roemer, following Meek. Walter (1977) represents a relatively minor financial change of direction for school parochiaid, though it may in time come to have wider implications.]

TWA

In Trans World Airlines (TWA) v Hardison, 1977, the Court ruled (7-2) that Title 7 of the Civil Rights Act (CRA) of 1964 as amended did not require a company to ignore a seniority system or to bear extra costs in order to accommodate an employee's religious beliefs—in this case a member of the sabbatarian Worldwide Church of God.

The CRA of 1964 primarily protected employment of "minority" people (e.g., blacks), but also enjoined discrimination on the basis of religion. The 1972 amendment incorporated into the act an administrative regulation requiring employers to make "reasonable" accommodations to the religious needs of employees.

The Court, speaking through Justice White, said that 1) the company did not have to go beyond a very minimal expense to accommodate a religious scruple, 2) the seniority system in the union's contract with the company did not discriminate against sabbatarians on the basis of their religion, and 3) the company should not be forced to discriminate against other employees who were not sabbatarians.

[The basic issue here was how far religious considerations must affect either the seniority provisions of a union contract or an employer's obligation to comply with the accommodation provision of the CRA. Not very far, said the Court: The act required only minimal concessions from the company or the union. According to the TWA ruling, the financial interest of the employer and the "religiously neutral" union contract protecting the vast majority of the workers took precedence over the religious expression of an individual worker.

[The Court's decision here seems closer in spirit to its separationist stance in McGowan (1961, Sunday closing) than to its accommodationism in Sherbert (1963, sabbatarian unemployment compensation) and in Yoder (1972, exemption from compulsory schooling.)

[The case has possible implications for education. Members of the Worldwide Church of God who work for school districts have brought similar suits against their employers. In one instance the district did not rehire a teacher who insisted on observing the sect's religious holidays; in two other places, teachers were fired for the same reason. The U.S. Department of Justice has filed suits in behalf of two of these people.

[A related issue is whether employees of a sectarian school are entitled to the benefits of the Fair Labor Standards Act of 1938. The Secretary of Labor brought suit against Seventh-day Adventist schools to force compliance with the act. At issue was equal pay for women teachers vs. sectarian school teach-

*ing (even of secular subjects) as a religious activity. In 1977, the parties
settled the dispute after a lower court ruling that favored the government.
Also, in 1976, the Supreme Court denied certiorari to an appeal from a federal
appeals court ruling that priests were not necessarily entitled to pay equal to
that of lay professors at a Catholic college. One issue was free exercise, but
the lower court refused to interfere with matters of church discipline.*

*[In addition, the NLRB has brought before the Supreme Court two Illinois
cases in which sectarian school authorities refused an NLRB order to negotiate
with unions as required by the National Labor Relations Act. A similar dispute
between the NLRB and an association of Catholic teachers in Pennsylvania is also before the courts.]*

Walter

In Wolman v Walter, 1977, the Court approved a variety of Ohio practices relating to nonpublic schools: a) the loan of textbooks (6-3); b) the financing
of state-supplied testing (6-3); c) subsidies for diagnostic testing by public
employees on the private school's premises (8-1); and d) remedial and counseling services off the school premises (7-2). The Court also disapproved grants
for e) instructional materials and equipment even when ostensibly loaned to
pupils or their parents (9-0); and f) pupil field trips (6-3).

Giving prevailing opinions, Justice Blackmun said that if the state sup-
plied standardized tests (e.g., achievement tests) and related test-scoring
services to public schools—item (b) above——then it might also provide them to
nonpublic schools. Diagnostic work—item (c)—included speech, hearing, and
psychological testing. Such services, said Blackmun, had "little or no educational content," and might be treated like the testing services.[p.244] The
Court felt that the diagnostic services did not "provide the same opportunity
for the transmission of sectarian views" as the other services did.[p.244]

The Court approved the state law's distinction between diagnostic and corrective services: In the case of corrective services, the inherent opportunity
for ideological indoctrination was greater. This was particularly important,
since nearly all the schools affected by the act were religious: In 1974-75,
Blackman noted, more than 96% of the state's nonpublic school pupils attended
sectarian schools and more than 92% at Catholic schools. Thus, Ohio had to insure that therapeutic, remedial, and guidance counseling services—item (d)—
would pass three tests: They must be performed by public employees, must be
open to public school pupils at the same place, and must be on "neutral" sites
—a public school, a public center, or even a mobile unit parked near the nonpublic school.

Textbooks—item (a)—primarily benefited the pupils, who could use them at
home as well as at school. But materials (wall maps, charts, etc.) and equipment—item (e)—primarily benefited the school and were generally stored there.
The Court had approved textbook loans earlier, in Allen (1968), but had struck
down direct aid to sectarian schools for materials and equipment, in Meek
(1975).

Busing for field trips—item (f)—was a new issue. The Court disallowed it
because, unlike busing in Everson (1947), it required specially scheduled buses
to serve trips whose essential aspects (destination, timing, classroom rele-

vance) were all controlled by the nonpublic school as part of its educational program. Therefore, the busing would benefit the schools more directly than the children.

While Blackmun announced the Court's decisions and while each part of his opinion expressed the views of a majority of the justices, only one other justice joined him in every part of his opinion, and alignments shifted. Concurring opinions, concurring but partially dissenting, and completely dissenting opinions abounded on each issue. Nearly all the justices applied the threefold test enunciated in _Lemon_: secular purpose, neutral primary effect, and minimal involvement.

[Three days after _Walter_, the Court as usual vacated other judgments of lower federal courts and remanded them for reconsideration in light of the new ruling: two from New York and one from Minnesota.

[On the one hand, this decision picked up the broken thread of aid to sectarian school pupils. The _Walter_ ruling on the Ohio law opened new areas of permissible parochiaid by making several distinctions:

[First, _Levitt_ (1973) had disallowed reimbursement for "state-mandated" testing. _Walter_ distinguished between teacher-prepared tests and state-supplied tests and approved funds for the latter. Second, _Meek_ had struck down such "auxiliary services" as guidance counseling for sectarian schools. _Walter_ distinguished between on-the-premises counseling and off-the-premises services and approved the latter. An underlying assumption in _Walter_ was similar to that of _Zorach_ (1952), the released time religious education case. If the potentially entangling practice (released time, test preparation, use of loaned materials, and remedial and counseling services) took place off the school premises, the state might accommodate them with public support.

[Third, in _Meek_, diagnostic testing had not been separated from therapeutic and remedial services. But in a footnote to its dicta, the Court had said that it might approve diagnostic testing alone as "general welfare" rather than as an auxiliary educational service. _Walter_ followed up on that distinction.

[On the other hand, although these rulings in _Walter_ provided some new financial aid or relief to sectarian schools and to their parents (indirectly, through the children), the biggest burdens—teacher salaries, equipment and materials purchases, and tuition charges—remained. Thus, both friends and foes of parochiaid claimed victory.

[Incidentally, a recent survey by the Department of Health, Education, and Welfare indicated that in the 1976-77 school year, about 75% of the country's nonpublic schools participated in federal ESEA programs and over 55% had federal lunch and special milk programs. These figures are in addition to state and local programs that aid nonpublic schools, their pupils, or parents in such areas as transportation, textbook loans, and health and other services.]

Johnson

In _Johnson_ v _Huntington_ _Beach_, 1977, the Court refused to review, and let stand, a California court ruling that the school could not recognize a student Bible study group by allowing it to use school classrooms and bulletin boards.

APPENDIX A - QUESTIONNAIRE

According to the U.S. Supreme Court*, the Constitution
implies that—

	Unlawful	Not unlawful	No ruling

A. The following public school practices relating to pupils are

	Unlawful	Not unlawful	No ruling
1. Studying the Bible	—	—	—
2. Studying about religion	—	—	—
3. Saying an interfaith prayer	—	—	—
4. Providing time and space for voluntary prayer	—	—	—
5. Distribution of free Bibles by Gideons	—	—	—
6. A moment of silent meditation at beginning of day	—	—	—
7. Singing patriotic songs that express belief in God	—	—	—
8. Christmas decorations, songs, stories, and plays	—	—	—
9. Dismissed-time voluntary religious education programs off school premises	—	—	—
10. Released-time voluntary religious education programs on school premises	—	—	—
11. Requiring teaching "creation by design" as an alternative theory to evolution	—	—	—
12. Inculcation of moral values	—	—	—
13. Inculcation of moral values via the Bible	—	—	—
14. Prohibiting sacrilegious movies	—	—	—
15. Baccalaureate services for graduating classes	—	—	—
16. Making up on Saturdays school days lost by snow or strikes	—	—	—
17. Requiring the flag salute, with no religious exemptions	—	—	—
18. Requiring vaccinations, with no religious exemptions	—	—	—
19. Requiring schooling to age 16, with no religious exemptions	—	—	—
20. Taking a religious census	—	—	—

B. The following practices relating to public school teachers are

	Unlawful	Not unlawful	No ruling
21. Requiring a teacher to be patriotic and of good moral character	—	—	—
22. Prohibiting teachers from teaching what is harmful to the public welfare	—	—	—
23. Requiring teachers to profess belief in a Supreme Being	—	—	—

---

*What do these words imply: How much effect does the Court's decision have?
Its opinions? Its refusal to hear an appeal from a lower court decision?

79

24. Restricting clothing and symbols worn by nuns teaching in public school   — — —

25. Requiring school districts to allow teachers time off for religious holidays   — — —

C. The following practices relating to sectarian schools are

26. Providing public funds for busing pupils to school   — — —

27. Public funds for busing pupils to museums   — — —

28. Public funds for secular textbooks   — — —

29. Public funds for wall maps and charts   — — —

30. Public funds for building maintenance and repair   — — —

31. Public funds for laboratory equipment   — — —

32. Public funds for state-mandated record keeping and reports   — — —

33. Public funds for state-mandated teacher-prepared testing   — — —

34. Public funds for state-supplied tests and scoring   — — —

35. Public funds for psychological testing by public employees on school premises   — — —

36. Public funds for therapeutic counseling by public employees on school premises   — — —

37. Public funds for salaries of teachers of secular subjects   — — —

38. Public funds for tuition reimbursement to parents   — — —

39. Public funds for vouchers for tuition   — — —

40. Granting tax-credit aids to parents   — — —

41. Leasing sectarian school rooms for public school classes jointly attended by pupils of both schools   — — —

42. Granting property tax exemptions for sectarian schools   — — —

43. Shared time (dual enrollment), for pupils to attend both schools part time   — — —

44. Tax exemptions for sectarian schools that practice racial discrimination   — — —

45. Requiring a state to provide funds for parochiaid that the U.S. Supreme Court has approved   — — —

46. Public standards for nonpublic school instruction   — — —

D. The following higher education practices are

    47. Teaching the Bible as literature at a state college   — — —

    48. Compulsory ROTC training, with no religious exemptions   — — —

    49. A church-supported chair in religion at a state college   — — —

    50. Compulsory chapel attendance at federal military academies   — — —

    51. Tax-free bonding for nonreligious buildings at church-related colleges, with no state guarantee   — — —

    52. State funds for unspecified secular purposes at church-related liberal arts colleges   — — —

    53. Federal funds for a college building that might, after twenty years, become a chapel   — — —

E. The following practices, indirectly related to education, are

    54. Restricting a person's freedom to preach or practice his/her religion   — — —

    55. Government aid to all religions, as opposed to aiding only one religion   — — —

    56. Governmental accommodation to religion, as opposed to strict neutrality   — — —

    57. Requiring membership in a sect for a religious exemption from compulsory military service   — — —

    58. Requiring membership in a sect for a religious exemption from compulsory high school attendance   — — —

ANSWERS TO QUESTIONNAIRE

No.	Supreme Court's comment	Case reference	Page
1	Not unlawful	Schempp	38
2	Not unlawful	Schempp	38
3	Unlawful	Engel	36
4	Unlawful	Netcong	57
5	No ruling	(Gideons)*	34
6	No ruling	(Schempp)	38
7	Not unlawful	Engel	36
8	No ruling	(Chamberlin)	42
9	Not unlawful	Zorach	31
10	Unlawful	McCollum	29
11	No ruling	(Brown)	47
12	Not unlawful	Pierce	21
13	Unlawful	Schempp	38
14	Unlawful	Burstyn	33
15	No ruling	(Chamberlin)	42
16	No ruling	(Yoder)	63
17	Unlawful	Barnette	24
18	Not unlawful	Jacobson	17
19	Unlawful	Yoder	63
20	No ruling	(Chamberlin)	42
21	Not unlawful	Pierce	21
22	Not unlawful	Pierce	21
23	Unlawful	Torcaso	36
24	No ruling		
25	No ruling	(TWA)	76
26	Not unlawful	Everson	26
27	Unlawful	Walter	77
28	Not unlawful	Allen	45
29	Unlawful	Meek	72
30	Unlawful	Nyquist	68
31	Unlawful	Meek	72
32	Unlawful	Nyquist	68
33	Unlawful	Walter	77
34	Not unlawful	Walter	77
35	Not unlawful	Walter	77
36	Unlawful	Walter	77
37	Unlawful	Lemon	57
38	Unlawful	Wolman	65
39	No ruling	(Lemon)	57
40	Unlawful	Nyquist	68
41	Not unlawful	Hartington	66
42	Not unlawful	Walz	55
43	No ruling	(Lemon)	57
44	No ruling	(Norwood)	67
45	Unlawful	Brusca	62

*Parentheses indicate either that the Court refused to hear an appeal of a lower court ruling or that the question is mentioned in our discussion of a related case.

46	Not unlawful	Meyer	19
47	No ruling	(Calvary Bible)	47
48	Not unlawful	Hamilton	23
49	No ruling		
50	Unlawful	Anderson	66
51	Not unlawful	Hunt	71
52	Not unlawful	Roemer	74
53	Unlawful	Tilton	60
54	Not unlawful	Reynolds	17
55	Unlawful	Everson	26
56	Not unlawful	Sherbert	42
57	Unlawful	Welsh	49
58	Not unlawful	Yoder	63

APPENDIX B - SOME ISSUES FOR DISCUSSION
(NOTE: See also list of areas of church-state interaction, page 10.)

1. Public Schools: Practices Related to Religion

Morning devotions: prayers, Bible reading, hymns? (see Engel, Schempp)

"Religious" readings? (see Schempp, Netcong)

Provide time and/or facilities for meditation?
For voluntary, pupil-initiated prayer? (see Netcong, Schempp)

Require pledge of allegiance to flag by everyone? (see Barnette)

School-approved Bible study club on school premises? (see Johnson)

Pupil-led religion club, not during school hours:
Sectarian?
Interfaith?
For academic study of religion?

Transcendental Meditation (see Schempp):
Elective course? (see McCollum)
Teacher-led voluntary group or club?

Display religious symbols:
In classrooms? On windows?
Elsewhere on premises? (see Lowe)

Distribute Bible (Gideon or other) on school premises? (see Gideons)

Distribute religious literature on school premises:
Not during school hours?
Not by school personnel?
Display on student-run bulletin board? (see Johnson)

In primary grade classrooms:
Grace before "milk and cookies"? (see DeKalb)
Post Sunday School attendance chart?
Use children's religious magazine?

Check on religious school attendance of pupils:
During released or dismissed time?
When excused for religious observance?

Religious census of pupils?

Collect money for poor children abroad, funneled through missionary enterprise?

Require vaccination?
Use fluoridated water?
Religiously offensive food in cafeteria?

Recognize religious and quasi-religious holidays with songs, plays, stories, displays (see Chamberlin):
Christmas? Easter? Hanukkah? Halloween? Thanksgiving?

Voluntary baccalaureate exercises (clergy, sermon, etc.) for graduates:
In school? In a church? In a public building? (see Chamberlin)

Invocations and benedictions at school dedications, banquets, and other exercises? At school activities not on school premises? (see Wiest)

84

2. Public Schools: Curriculum (for two special books, see Preface, page 1)

Teaching about religion (see Schempp, McCollum):
    Separate unit/course or where relevant to other course material?
    Religious issues in sciences and humanities? Critical thinking?
    Experiential learning? Visits to churches?

Bible as textbook (see Schempp):
    Is it sectarian? (see discussion, page 13)
    As religious document or as literature?
    For historic interest or impact on modern society?
    Within literature or social studies course, or as separate subject?
    "Just like Shakespeare" in literature course?
    For moral instruction or "objective" approach?

Who teaches:
    Religious representatives? As guests? As resources for teachers?
    Regular teacher, but specially trained?

Decisions about materials and methods:
    By teacher? Curriculum specialist? Panel of religious leaders? Admin-
    istrators? Parents? Pupils?

Compulsory attendance at religion/Bible course or unit?

Teach "moral and spiritual values"? (see Welsh)

Teach evolution (see Epperson)
    Germ theory?
    "Worldliness"? (see Yoder)

Require participation:
    Gym? Dance classes? Music? Short-sleeved dresses?

Censorship of sacrilegious materials? (see Burstyn)

Guest speakers:
    Evangelizers, Satanists, atheists, unpopular sects?

3. Public Schools: Calendar

Close for religious holidays:
    Good Friday? Jewish High Holy Days? Others?
    Excuse absences if school not closed? (see Zorach)
    Limit number of excused religious absences? (see TWA)

School-sponsored activities, in school or outside:
    Conflicting with religious holidays?
    On Sunday?
    Conflicting with religious school after regular hours?

Interference with Christian sabbatarians and Orthodox Jews (see Sherbert):
    School-sponsored enrichment activities on Saturday?
    Making up on Saturdays days lost by snow or strikes?
    College entrance examinations on Saturday?
    Graduation exercises on Friday evening?
    Similar questions about Friday for Moslems?

Compulsory school attendance? Age limit? (see Yoder, Donner)

85

4. Public Schools: Faculty

Criteria for selection, tenure, promotion, dismissal:
    Moral? Patriotic? Religious? (see Pierce, Torcaso)

Clergy or nuns as teachers:
    Religious garb? Emblems on clothing?

Limitations on absences for religious reasons? (see TWA)

Non-participation in school activities for religious reasons (gym, dances, etc.)?

Restrictions on teacher's religious expression? (see Reynolds)

Observing unusual religious practices (e.g., not cutting hair)?

Blasphemy, in states where it is a crime? (see Burstyn)

Conducting (or attending) voluntary devotional service on school premises but outside regular hours?

Advisor to religious "study" group or club:
    On school premises?
    Organized in school, but meeting off premises?
    Sectarian? Interfaith? Nonsectarian?

Training (and certification):
    To handle "religious" subject matter?
    To deal with "moral and spiritual" issues?

5. Public Schools: Miscellaneous

Clergy (or others) chosen to represent religious groups or religious points of view on school policy committees?

Rules for use/rental/lease of school buildings for religious purposes outside of school hours?

6. Sectarian Schools

Obligations to government's interest in education and the general welfare (and rights vis-a-vis the government) (see Pierce, Meyer):
    Curriculum standards? Health and safety? Attendance? Finances?
    Free exercise of religion? Parents' rights?

A state "Office for Nonpublic Education"?

Separability of secular activities, versus religious permeation? (see Allen, Lemon, Nyquist, Meek, Walter)

Definition of "parochiaid"? (see page 14)
    Criteria for permissible parochiaid? (see Lemon)

Public funds for busing:
    To and from school? (see Everson)
    For field trips? (see Walter)

Textbooks? (see Cochran, Allen)
    Magazines, wall maps, etc.? (see Meek)

Grants, tuition reimbursements, and/or tax credits? (see Wolman, Nyquist)

Tax exemptions (property tax, income tax, charitable contributions)? (see Walz, Norwood, Runyon)
  Disallowance for racial discrimination?

State purchase of secular services from the school (see Lemon, Nyquist, Walter):
  State-mandated testing, record keeping, and reporting?
  Building maintenance?
  Materials and equipment? (see Meek)
  Salaries of teachers of secular subjects (math, science, vocational ed., driver ed., physical ed., sports)?

State funds for auxiliary educational services:
  On school premises or off?
  Health and safety—nurses, doctors, equipment?
  Diagnostic—speech, hearing, reading, psychological?
  Remedial and counseling?

Vouchers for tuition?

Lease church or school rooms for public school classes? (see Hartington)
  Restriction on decor—religious pictures/symbols?

Shared time: sectarian school children in public school for secular subjects?

Reversed shared time: public school pupils (and teachers) in sectarian schools for secular subjects?

Shared personnel?

Joint purchasing?

ESEA of 1965 benefits (for educationally deprived, including sectarian school pupils):
  Who selects pupils and materials? And how? (see Flast)
  Who administers: public personnel only?
  Where: away from sectarian school premises? (see Hartington)
  When: (see "Public Schools: Calendar," above)?

Labor relations:
  May teachers unionize and demand negotiations: Nuns? Priests? Laity?
  May lay teachers participate in state teacher retirement plan?

7. Higher Education

Public funds for sectarian colleges (see Tilton, Roemer):
  Theological schools vs. church-related "liberal arts" colleges?
  For secular activities?
  For buildings?
  For research?
  Through urban renewal?
  Through war surplus transfers?

At state colleges:
  Religion and Bible literature courses? (see Calvary Bible)
  Compulsory ROTC? (see Hamilton)
  Military academies—compulsory chapel attendance? (see Anderson)

NDEA/GI Bill benefits: to sectarian colleges, seminaries, for vocation?

8. General Considerations

What other issues have been raised? Might or should be raised?

Are these issues legal, moral, or both?

In case of conflict, which governs: Under what circumstances is a person's duty to ultimate values/God higher than to state and society?

In what sense can/should the government be "neutral" in religious matters?

Is religious liberty different in kind from freedom of speech and of the press?

Criteria and limits for separation of church and state? For cooperation?

Relation between free exercise of religion and freedom from religion (no establishment)?

Relation between religious liberty and other goals of American society—national unity, common defense, domestic tranquility, general welfare? (see discussion, page 9.)

Definitions: Religion? Moral values? Spiritual values? (see Welsh)
How are they related?
What are the sanctions?

Does America have a civic "religion"? What are the responsibilities of education in this area?

In what sense, if any, is this a Christian country? A religious country?
What are the implications for education?

How far must the majority go to accommodate the minority(ties)? Or must a minority go to cater to the majority? To what extent, if at all, does it depend on the size of the minority?

For people who object to the public school's secularity or to its accommodations to religion, how available and practical are alternatives?

To what extent do peer pressure and official sanction counteract a young child's privilege of exemption from a religious practice?
His/her freedom to practice a nonconforming religion?
Same questions for teachers—in school? In society?

Goals of education? Their source?

9. First Amendment Religion Clauses; The Supreme Court

1. Congress shall make no law

Does that mean only Congress, and that state (and municipal) authorities may make such laws?

Does it mean only a negative prohibition against making certain kinds of laws, or are there positive implications for governmental authorities?

Is the prohibition absolute or limited?

2. Respecting an establishment of religion

Does this mean any more than if it read "Congress shall make no law establishing religion"?

Does this mean "separation of church and state"?

Does it mean no establishment of only one sect exclusively, of all Christian sects, of all religion?

What constitutes establishment—direct governmental support, indirect support, primary or incidental support, major or minor support?

Does religion mean sectarian membership, a theology, and cultic practices; or may it have none of these—a "secular religion"?

3. <u>Prohibiting the free exercise thereof</u>

Does "exercise" mean belief, verbal expression (oral or written) and advocacy, actions, or all three?

Is the prohibition absolute or limited?

Again, what does religion mean?

4. <u>Or</u>

What if the two clauses conflict——when to avoid supporting religion means to limit free exercise, or to avoid harming free exercise of religion means to give it support?

Does no establishment mean only no interference with free exercise?

5. When the Supreme Court—

Invalidates a practice, what can, should, must a state do about the decision? The proponents and/or opponents of the practice?

Refuses to review a case, what does it mean to the litigants? For similar cases in other states?

Expresses an opinion beyond the decision rendered in the case, what effect does the opinion have?

Declares that a practice does not violate the Constitution, what if the practice does violate the state constitution?

(Some legal terms used in this book and useful for further reading)

Absent (used as a preposition): in the absence of.

Absolute: without exception; governing in all cases; unconditional.

Accommodationist: one who, deferring to the importance of religion in our society, favors some governmental concessions to religion. Opposed to **separationist**: one who favors a minimum of interaction between government and religion.

Act: a law passed by the Congress or a state legislature; a statute.

Action: a court/judicial proceeding, in which one party prosecutes another for the enforcement or protection of a right, for the redress or prevention of a wrong, or for punishment of a public offense. Rough synonyms: suit, case, trial, litigation.

Adduce: to present as evidence or as an example.

Admission: an agreement to the opposition's claim, in order to reduce the number of facts or allegations to be proved; similar to stipulation.

Advocate: to speak in favor of.

Affirm: to declare a lower court's judgment valid and correct.

A fortiori ("with more strength"; AY fore-SHO-righ; used as an adverbial conjunction): more certainly. It describes a conclusion based on an earlier, accepted conclusion: e.g., if three are too many, a fortiori four are too many.

Amicus, amicus curiae ("friend of the court"; a-MIGH-cus KYU-ri-ee, or a-MEE-cus KOO-ree-igh): a person not a party to the suit who is allowed to add an argument to the proceedings, an amicus brief.

Appeal: a complaint to a higher court of an alleged injustice or error in a lower court's decision. **Appellant**: one who appeals. **Appellee**: the opposite side, respondent. Similar to plaintiff and defendant.

Appellate court, court of appeals: a state or federal court that may review the judgment of a lower court. In a **trial de novo**, the appeals court may also hear new evidence or redetermine the facts that appear in the record of the original trial.

    The U.S. Supreme Court is the final court of appeals. Most cases reach the Supreme Court by appeal of the losing side in a lower court (usually a federal court or a state supreme court), provided that the Supreme Court agrees to accept the case and issues a writ of certiorari.

Auxiliary services: diagnostic, testing, therapeutic, remedial, and counseling services to pupils. Public funding of such services in nonpublic schools is a subject of dispute.

Bill: a proposed law.

Bill of Rights: the first ten amendments to the U.S. Constitution.

Brief: a statement of proposed arguments to be used by a lawyer in an appellate court.

Case: an action.

Certiorari ("certified"; SIR-sho-RARE-igh, or SIR-sho-RAH-ree): a writ granting an appellate proceeding in order to reexamine a lower court's decision. Deny certiorari: to refuse to consider a case; to deny an appeal
 or a hearing. (See let stand, below.)

Challenge: to object or take exception to.

Cite: to support an argument or decision by referring to legal authorities and
 precedents. Citations from court reports and other references follow a
 standard form: volume number, title of series, page number, and year:
 e.g., 50 US 453 (1965). If there are two page numbers in the citation, the
 first usually identifies the case or chapter and the second is the page
 quoted. (See report, below.)(In a Court citation, the year is the term.)

Class action: a suit brought on behalf of oneself and others who are in the
 same situation.

Clause: a subdivision of a legal document, especially of an amendment to the
 Constitution.

Common law: the part of English common law (as opposed to Roman law or canon
 law) that was in force in the American colonies and is still part of U.S.
 law.

Complaint: a pleading by a plaintiff/complainant that initiates a civil action.

Concurring opinion: see opinion.

Constitutional: consistent with or authorized by the constitution; or not
 conflicting with any part of it—in which case the law or practice is
 "not unconstitutional."

Construe: to determine the sense or "real meaning" of obscurities or ambigu-
 ities in a document. Construction: the result of construing. (See also
 strict construction, below.)

Count: a charge, one of the offenses in the plaintiff's stated causes for an
 action.

Decide: to judge, hold, rule, declare, determine, find. Decision: a judgment, holding, ruling, declaration, determination, finding, disposition.
 The court's decision may be summary (see below) or may be the result of
 a hearing and accompanied by an opinion (see below). Contrast dictum.

De minimis: ("about trifles"—the law does not care; dee MIN-i-mees): of no
 concern to the law.

Deprive: to take without consent.

Dictum, obiter dictum (plural: dicta; "other remarks"): that part of an opinion that comments on some aspect of the case, as distinct from the actual
 decision for or against the defendant/respondent.

Dissenting opinion: see opinion.

Distinguish: to point out an essential difference between the case at hand and
 a previous case, such that the earlier decision does not apply here.

Doctrine: a principle, standard, basic or general rule or criterion, theory,
 or tenet of law which is pronounced (announced, enunciated, etc.) by the
 Court for deciding issues.

Equal protection of the law: the equal access to courts; to life, liberty, property, and pursuit of happiness; and subject to no special restrictions or burdens.

Error: a mistake in law or in application of law that warrants reversal in appellate court.

Ex parte ("in behalf of"; ex PAR-teh): in the title of a case where no adversary is named, refers to the party that brought the action.

Ex rel ("in relation to"): in the title of a case, indicates proceedings initiated by the state in behalf of an individual.

Federal courts (principal ones): District court, a trial court of original jurisdiction. Court of appeal (or appellate court; formerly, circuit court), with three or more judges (see appellate court, above). Supreme Court, usually appellate; a justice may participate in the work of a lower court in his/her assigned district.

Finding: a court's decision—as to the facts in a case, an interpretation of the facts, or the case as a whole.

Framers (of the Constitution; also called fathers): members of the constitutional convention. To arrive at the original intent of the framers, jurists often consult the Federalist Papers, written by Madison, Hamilton, and Jay to explain and advocate the Constitution during the ratification controversies.

Frivolous appeal: one obviously devoid of merit, presenting no substantive question for judgment.

Illicit: unlawful, illegal.

In re ("in the matter of"): in the title of a case, usually indicates that it is not an adversary proceeding, but merely asking for a judgment about some matter.

Intervenor-defendant: a party whom the judge allows to enter the case as a co-defendant, who may represent different interests, and who may appeal the decision if the original defendant refuses to do so. In such instances, the name that appears in the title of the Supreme Court case may be different from that in the lower court case.

Join an opinion: to sign or agree with another judge/justice's opinion, agreeing with both the conclusion and the reasoning; distinguished from concurring, which agrees only with the conclusion. (See opinion, below.)

Justice: a judge in the Supreme Court (and in some state appellate courts). The nine justices are appointed for life by the President, subject to Senate approval.

Let stand: to deny certiorari of an appeal, in which case the lower court's decision stands. This is an imprecise journalistic term which describes the effect of the denial but not the purpose. The Court's refusal of an appeal indicates neither approval nor disapproval of the lower court's decision.

Majority opinion: see opinion.

Moot case: one that does not deal with existing facts or rights (usually because of changed circumstances) and is therefore not worth deciding.

Obiter dictum/a: see dictum.

Opinion: a judge/justice's decision about the case accompanied by discussion of the law, principles involved, and reasons for the decision.
   Majority opinion: one that is agreed to by the majority participating. It speaks for the Court and gives both its decision and official reasoning. Unless otherwise noted, a justice is presumed to agree.
   Concurring opinion: one that agrees with the decision of the prevailing side but for different reasons.
   Dissenting opinion: one that disagrees with the majority's conclusion, together with reasons for the dissent.
   Plurality/prevailing opinion: one that declares the majority decision but, with no majority opinion, gives the opinion of only the greatest number who agree. Thus, no opinion speaks officially for the Court.
   Per curiam opinion: a unanimous but anonymous opinion of the Court.

Ordinance: a municipal law.

Parochiaid: see discussion of this term, on page 14.

Passive role: the Court's tendency to refrain from judgment on a practice, statute, or issue and to leave legislative acts undisturbed; as opposed to an active role for the Court.

Peremptory decision: one handed down without explanation. (See summarily, below.)

Plaintiff: the party that brings the action in the trial court. Defendant: the party against whom the action is brought. An appellant is called a "plaintiff in error."

Police power: a state's power to make and enforce laws for the general welfare of the public—including regulation of education, both public and nonpublic.

Proceeding: an action; also called judicial proceeding/s.

Purchase of services: the granting of state funds to sectarian schools for "secular, non-ideological" equipment, supplies, and activities (e.g., building maintenance, testing, record keeping, and salaries).

Record: the history of the suit, from beginning to end, as furnished to the appellate court. Generally, appellants may not go outside those items introduced in evidence in the lower court.

Rehear: to reconsider a case for possible error in the earlier trial or appeal.

Remand: to send the case back to the previous court, usually after a reversal, for some action by that court—a new trial or a new ruling.

Reports: Actions, decisions, and opinions of the Supreme Court are officially published in the United States Reports (cited as ___US___). Before 1875 they were identified by the name of the reporter: e.g., Peters, Howard, Wallace (cited as __Pet___).
   The Supreme Court Reporter (cited as ___SCt___) and Lawyer's Edition (cited as ___LEd___ or as ___LEd2d___, the second series having begun with 1956) are privately published. They appear shortly after the Court acts, as paper bound booklets. Later, when the U.S. Report is published, these two private publications insert page references to the U.S. Report and republish in hard cover.

The Federal Reporter (cited as ___F___) records for U.S. courts of appeal, and the Federal Supplement (cited as ___FSupp___) for U.S. district courts. Records of state supreme courts are found in regional reports (e.g., Atlantic Reporter, cited as ___A___) as well as in individual state reports. Some proceedings of these lower appeals courts are not reported, though the original trial record is available.

Respondent: the party that contends against an appeal; appellee.

Reverse: to contradict the previous court's decision; usually accompanied by a remand to the lower court for reconsideration in the light of the new decision and the principles mentioned in the opinion.

Sect: any religious denomination, mainstream or divergent.

Separationist: see accommodationist.

Standing: a right to sue.

Stare decisis ("stand by what has been decided"; STAY-ree or STAH-reh de-SIGH-sis): adhering to precedent, applying a previous decision to the present case; the previous decision has become the rule.

Stipulated facts: facts that have been agreed to by an opposing party without having been "discovered" by adversary methods. Similar to an admission. Usually, the record before the appellate court contains fewer details in such cases.

Strict construction: sticking to the letter of the Constitution, not recognizing anything that has not been explicitly expressed. Opposed to liberal construction: expanding the literal meaning of what is written so as to apply the Constitution to a particular case—provided that the interpretation is not inconsistent with the language.

These two terms are often used imprecisely. Strict construction is sometimes held to be closer to the framers' specific intentions in their own situation, while liberal construction is claimed to represent the spirit of the framers as it should be transferred to the later situation. Both sides appeal to the Federalist Papers (see framers, above).

Other people more loosely apply the two terms to the passive and active roles of the Court (see passive role, above).

Summarily: without a hearing. The Court may summarily affirm or reverse a lower court's decision (thus rendering a peremptory decision), or it may summarily grant or deny certiorari. Such a summary (or "memorandum") disposition of an appeal may or may not be accompanied by an explanation of, or the dissents from, the Court's action.

Term: The "fall term" of the Court usually extends from early October through the following July. During the term the Court receives briefs, hears arguments, studies cases, confers and decides upon the writing of opinions, and hands down decisions.

Theory: see doctrine.

Unanimous: with the agreement of all the justices participating, or with no dissents.

NOTE: The standard reference is Black's Law Dictionary, West Publishing Co., St. Paul, Minn.

APPENDIX D – INDEX OF U.S. SUPREME COURT CASES

---

*Not argued before the Supreme Court [see lower court citation for report]
**Not reported in the record of the lower court of appeals